IRELAND'S RAILWAY HERITAGE
THE RAILWAYS OF
LEINSTER

IRELAND'S RAILWAY HERITAGE
THE RAILWAYS OF
LEINSTER

MICHAEL H. C. BAKER

• A SILVER LINK BOOK •

from

○ *The* CUMHA *Collection* ○

For Katreeya Maeve Baker

© Michael H. C. Baker 2008

All rights reserved. No part of this publication may be reproduced, stored in a retrieval system or transmitted, in any form or by any means, electronic, mechanical, photocopying, recording or otherwise, without prior permission in writing from Silver Link Publishing Ltd.

First published in 2008

British Library Cataloguing in Publication Data

A catalogue record for this book is available from the British Library.

ISBN 978 1 85895 247 5

Silver Link Publishing Ltd
The Trundle
Ringstead Road
Great Addington
Kettering
Northants NN14 4BW

Tel/Fax: 01536 330588
email: sales@nostalgiacollection.com
Website: www.nostalgiacollection.com

Printed and bound in Great Britain

The CUMHA Collection
is an imprint of Silver Link Publishing Ltd

Preserved 4-4-0 No 85 *Merlin*, complete with 'Enterprise' headboards, receives attention at Dundalk before heading for Dublin in August 2002. There were five of these magnificent-looking three-cylinder Compounds. Originally turned out in black, on their first overhaul they were repainted in a magnificent sky blue, and in 1932 were put in charge of the fastest ever Dublin-Belfast schedules. The average overall time, with five stops, was 2hr 28min, which, as E. M. Patterson pointed out in 1962, was 'just under the present non-stop diesel allowance.' *Merlin* has a Belpaire boiler, fitted in 1946-7.

Contents

Introduction and Acknowledgements	9
Across the border	11
Lines around Dundalk	13
Drogheda, Navan and branches	26
Malahide and Howth	37
Midland Great Western lines	43
Great Southern & Western lines	51
Waterford	71
Rosslare to Dublin	77
Dublin	
Harcourt Street	99
Terenure (Dublin & Blessington Tramway)	101
Westland Row/Pearse and the Loop Line	102
Amiens Street/Connolly and North Wall	105
Broadstone	114
Kingsbridge/Heuston	117
Inchicore	124
Index of photographic locations	128

Passengers and murals at Bray on a not particularly warm July day in 1986.

Ireland's Railway Heritage: Leinster

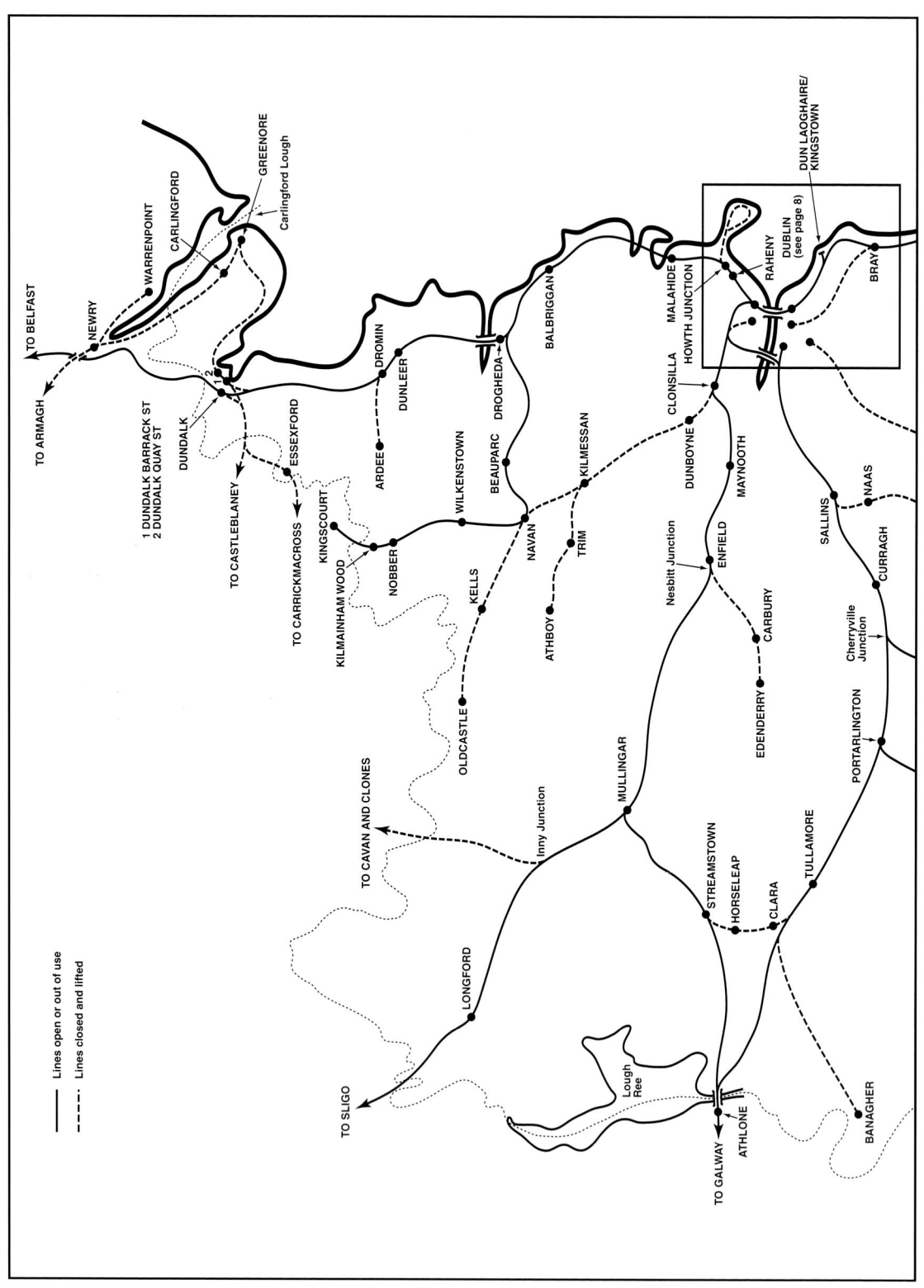

Ireland's Railway Heritage: Leinster

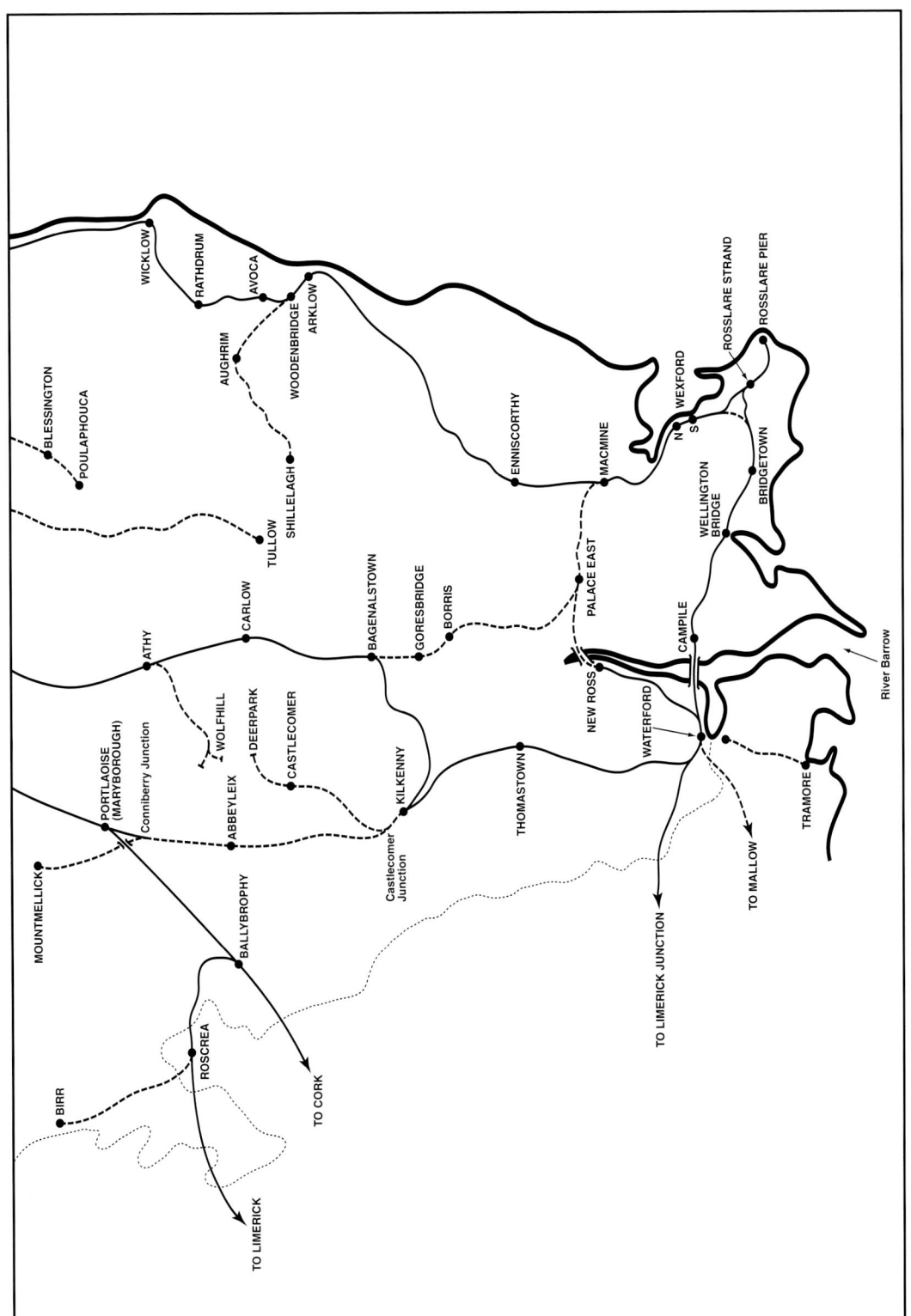

The railways of Leinster, showing principal stations and other locations mentioned in the book.

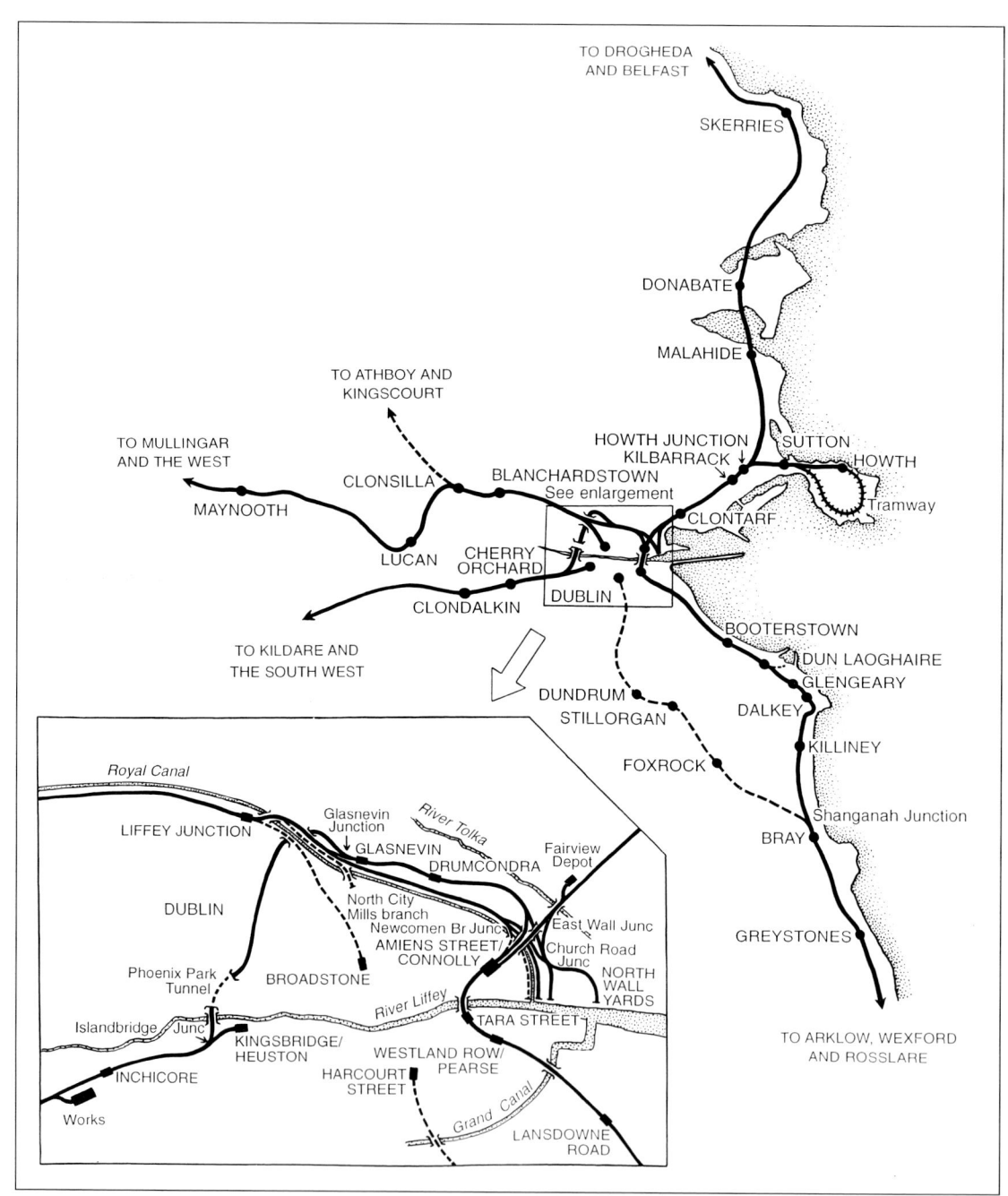

Railways of the Dublin area

Introduction and Acknowledgements

Leinster, one of Ireland's four provinces, is far and away the most populous by virtue of possessing Dublin, the capital of the Republic. Had this story been written half a century ago it would have been a somewhat downbeat one, for in those days rail travel was in decline. No branch line was seen as free from the threat of extinction, many had already gone and many more would follow, and although main-line traffic between Dublin and the major provincial towns was generally holding up, commuting in and out of Dublin by train was very much the exception rather than the rule. Indeed, one of the four commuter lines, that from Bray to Harcourt Street, was about to close, leaving intact just the former Dublin & South Eastern coastal route by way of Dun Laoghaire and the Great Northern Railway (GNR) lines from Dundalk and Howth. Virtually no-one came in to work (commuting was a term hardly in use in Ireland 50 years ago) by way of the former Great Southern & Western Railway (GSWR) main line from the south by way of Kildare, or the Midland Great Western Railway (MGWR) one from the Midlands and Mullingar. The last Dublin trams had gone, although the GNR Hill of Howth tram line was still functioning, and if you didn't use a car – and not many did – you either walked or went to work in the capital by bus. This latter, almost certainly a double-deck Leyland, was seen as the answer to Dublin's commuter problems, such as they were.

As the railway network of Leinster evolved Dublin inevitably dominated the picture, but there were many branch lines within the province that served small towns and villages distant from the capital. There were four main lines radiating from Dublin, all of which threw off branches. There was the GNR main line connecting Belfast and other parts of Ulster with Dublin; the Midland Great Western Railway linking Dublin with Mullingar, Athlone and the north-west and west coasts; the Great Southern & Western Railway, which came in from Limerick, Cork, Waterford and the west coast by way of Kildare; and the Dublin & South Eastern (D&SER), also serving Waterford and points east of there as well as the south-east coast from Rosslare by way of Wexford.

We will start in the far north, from what is now the border with the British-administered counties of Down, Antrim, Fermanagh, Tyrone, Londonderry and Armagh (not, strictly speaking, Ulster, for that province also includes Cavan, Donegal and Monaghan), and (shedding snow-shoes, fur coats and teams of huskies!) work our way down to the tropical south before heading back up to end our survey among the expansions, retractions and – once again, it is delightful to note – expansions of Ireland's capital, the powerhouse of that extraordinary phenomenon of the late 1990s and into the 21st century, the Celtic Tiger. Today Leinster has a population of 2,105, 579, of whom no fewer than 1,556,446 live in Greater Dublin.

There are a number of people to thank who have helped with photographs, with the text or in other ways. John Langford, Richard Casserley and Neil Sprinks have, as always, come up trumps with pictures from their extensive collections. I am most grateful to Tim Moriarty, the Librarian of the Irish Railway Record Society, for checking the introductory text, although I must emphasise that any errors are solely my responsibility. Michael Walsh, the IRRS Chairman, has been encouraging, and I am much indebted to many past and present members of the IRRS for their contributions to the society's Journal over the years, which provide such an invaluable source for anyone attempting to record aspects of the Irish railway scene. Other photographs have been passed on to me by members over the years; some from two friends who, sadly, have died recently, David Murray and Walter McGrath. Others are from elsewhere – the Hugh Davies collection is an invaluable source. Then there are those I have taken myself in the years since my first visit to Ireland in 1959.

So much has changed in those nearly 50 years. Steam could still be found at work in Leinster, particularly on the former GNR network, and I did manage one steam journey on CIE metals, between Waterford and Macmine Junction behind one of those wonderful '101' Class 0-6-0s that feature so prominently in the pages of this book. Not the least enjoyable aspect of my 2006 holiday on the shores of Carlingford Lough was to pop up to Belfast on the Saturday evening of our arrival and enjoy the spectacle of the 127-year-old '101' No 186 steaming into Belfast Central with what can only be described as a jaunty air, hauling the packed 'Portrush Flyer'. One can hardly over-praise the Railway Preservation Society of Ireland for what its members have achieved on both sides of the Border, from the earliest times when they were able to acquire steam locomotives and wooden-bodied carriages straight from service, through the dark decades of the 'Troubles', to the present, happier days of the 21st century.

Back in the 1970s and '80s I did quite a lot of cab journeys in and out of Heuston and Connolly stations, either in General Motors Bo-Bos or re-engined 'A' Class Co-Cos. These were often organised for me by Brian d'A. Paterson, CIE's Rail Control Officer, Personnel. He was a lovely man, a real gentleman who always made my wife, Maeve, and myself welcome in his office at Islandbridge. Whenever his name came up in conversation with drivers he was spoken of with respect and affection. Sadly he died of a heart attack while still in office. He had started his career way back, and in the 1940s had been assistant to A. P. Reynolds, the first Chairman of CIE, appointed in 1945. Reynolds was not a universally popular choice – his background was buses, and he had been in charge of Dublin United Transport Services, which operated Dublin's bus and tram network, a post he combined with that of head of the Great Southern between 1942 and 1945. Eventually, in 1949, following the publication of the Milne Report on the future of public transport in Eire, or the Republic of Ireland as it officially became that year, Reynolds was asked to resign. Statements that the public 'would not travel by train if any other form of transport was available' did not help his cause. Brian Paterson told me that Reynolds insisted on taking his severance pay 'in five pound notes in a leather bag', and that the last he had heard of him was that he was running a shop down on the Quays.

Those cab journeys were fascinating, chiefly for the stories the drivers, who had started their careers on steam, had to tell. Nearly all of them had connections with the UK, having either lived for a while in England, usually London, or having relations there. Knowing only too well the unhappy 800-year relationship of England and Ireland – so, you may think that, with a wife called Maeve, a mother-in-law who was a Gaelic scholar and a father-in law whose older brothers had fought both in the struggle for independence and the subsequent civil war, how could I have avoided the subject – I was constantly surprised by the friendliness of every railwayman I met.

The extraordinary prosperity of Ireland today is something to behold. One of the greatest beneficiaries, if somewhat belatedly, has been the rail network, particularly in the area around the capital, ie Leinster. Not only is commuter travel increasing apace with a new terminus down in the business area by the docks, new tracks added on the main line to the west out towards Kildare, new stations in the suburbs, extensions to the electrified DART network, and the possibility of closed lines being re-opened, but trams have also returned to the streets of Dublin, with extensions already planned, and an underground network is on the cards. The first decade of the 21st century is indeed a golden age for rail travel in Leinster.

Across the Border

The international main line, as it has been since the early 1920s, linking Ireland's two largest cities, Dublin and Belfast, was opened stage by stage – one might add, gauge by gauge – between 1839 and 1853. It leaves Ulster and enters Leinster high in the Armagh Hills, just south of the Slieve Gullion Forest Park and 575-metre-high Slieve Gullion itself. The station closest to the border in Ulster, 3 miles distant, was Adavoyle, which opened in 1892 and closed in 1933. Long ago there was a station a mile and a half south of the border, variously named Mount Pleasant, Plaster and Jonesborough. This opened in 1850, had a chequered existence and had finally expired by 1887, some 35 years before the border came into existence. Since then Dundalk, 5¼ miles to the south, has been the first station in Leinster.

The reference to more than one gauge comes about on account of the line from Belfast Great Victoria Street to Portadown originally being of the very odd gauge of 6ft 2in, the choice of the Ulster Railway. It was converted to 5ft 3in in 1847. Belfast to Portadown opened in 1842. The completion of the magnificent 140-foot-high, 18-arch Criagmore Viaduct in 1852 saw through trains operating to Newfoundwell, immediately north of Drogheda. Next year a temporary viaduct over the Boyne enabled through Dublin to Belfast trains to commence; two years later the permanent Boyne Viaduct, as spectacular in its way as the Criagmore one, came into use.

This picture illustrates the remoteness of the border country and the heavy engineering work involved in taking the line into the high hills between Newry and Dundalk. In August 2005 the 14.50 'Enterprise' from Dublin to Belfast is pictured a few hundred yards north of the border. The locomotive is General Motors 3200hp No 228 *River Owenea/An Abhainn Bhui*, newly repainted in the highly attractive green, yellow and silver livery designed to match IR's new generation of Spanish-built carriages, then just being delivered but not yet in public service.

The view from the cab of one of the re-engined '001' ('A') Class Co-Cos, built by Metropolitan Vickers in 1955-6, hauling the southbound 'Enterprise' as it approaches the border between the Republic of Ireland and Northern Ireland on a grey August day in 1984.

IRELAND'S RAILWAY HERITAGE: LEINSTER

Above The first northbound 'Enterprise' of the day, the 07.35 out of Dublin, approaching the border close to the site of the long-vanished Mount Pleasant station, 58 miles from Dublin, on a sunny July morning in 2006. The locomotive is one of the 3200hp 'River' Class Co-Cos built by General Motors of Ontario, Canada, in 1994-5, which haul practically all long-distance passenger trains in Ireland today.

Below left The same train, made up of De Dietrich stock, built in France in 1996 and bearing some resemblance to SNCF's TGV trains, curves away towards the border, with the Driving Brake 1st, complete with newly repainted all-yellow cab front, bringing up the rear.

The 'Enterprise' service is something of a 'curate's egg'. Jointly owned by Iarnrod Eireann and Translink NI Railways, neither its end-to-end schedule nor its timekeeping has really been as good as it should, but at least on the several occasions I observed it during the week-ending 5 August 2006 it appeared to be on its best behaviour as far as keeping to its 125-minute/113-mile schedule was concerned.

Below The two previous pictures were taken from this ornate cast-iron bridge, dating from 1850. There was a time, not so long ago, when one did not linger in these parts, especially with a camera sporting a telephoto lens hung around one's neck, beautiful though the scenery might be.

Lines around Dundalk

The first Dundalk station was opened by the Dublin & Belfast Junction Railway in 1849, the year the lines from Newfoundwell and Castleblaney arrived in the town, and was situated in the vee formed by the junction of the two lines. Castleblaney, 18 miles from Dundalk, was the junction of the lines to Clones, completed in 1858, and to Armagh, opened in 1910. This latter line was exceedingly short-lived, the Castleblaney to Keady section being shut by the GNR after a mere 13 years. Armagh to Keady was closed for passenger traffic at the beginning of 1932, goods surviving until 1957. Dundalk to Castleblaney and Clones was closed for passenger traffic by the GNR in 1957, and three years later, by now the property of CIE, it closed for goods too. We had best also mention the Inniskeen to Carrickmacross branch which, although, almost entirely in County Monaghan and therefore in Ulster, did have one station in Leinster, at Essexford. It was opened by the GNR in 1886 and closed to passengers during the fuel crisis in early 1947, never to open again; freight lasted until 1960. Essexford, the only intermediate station on the branch, got its name from Queen Elizabeth I's favourite earl, and did not open until a year or so after the branch began business, closing for a time in the mid-1920s. One can only conclude that it was not a money-spinner.

Many were the links between Irish and English railways, but none were as instantly recognisable as that between the Dundalk, Newry & Greenore Railway and the London & North Western Railway. The DN&GR began at Quay Street station, Dundalk, and ran eastwards along the shores of Dundalk Bay for 12½ miles to Greenore. Opened in 1873, a second line quickly followed three years later, from Greenore north-westwards on the other side of the peninsula and along the edge of Carlingford Lough for 14 miles to Newry. Wholly owned by the LNWR, it was therefore quite naturally equipped with standard Crewe and Wolverton products: a stable of Webb 0-6-0 saddle tanks, painted black, and a fleet of non-corridor purple-brown-and-spilt-milk six-wheel carriages. Few railways could match the scenery through which the company operated, virtually all of it along the water's edge; fittingly, its principal business was sending cattle by way of Greenore, a port it created, and Holyhead. Passenger steamers also plied the route, which was advertised as 'The Direct and Most Comfortable Route between London & Belfast and the North of Ireland'. The LNWR built a very grand hotel at Greenore and the village's two principal streets were named, just in case you still hadn't got the message, Anglesey Terrace and Euston Street.

Dundalk became one of the great railway towns of Ireland – indeed, size for size, probably the greatest – for the GNR opened its works here in 1881. By 1900 it had more than 1,000 employees, something like one-tenth of the town's population, and was known as 'the jewel in Dundalk's crown'. Like most railway towns it was not pretty, but for an enthusiast it was a most interesting place. Although the Dundalk, Newry & Greenore's tracks ended at Quay Street, its trains continued over GNR (originally Irish North Western) metals to Barrack Street, the most central of the town's three stations, past the Pork Factory siding, over the main Dublin to Belfast line at the celebrated Square Crossing and past the back of the Works to the West Junction on the Castleblaney line, where they reversed into the GNR main-line station. This, known as Dundalk Junction and renamed Clarke in 1966, was opened in 1893, replacing the original one and to the north of it, and is a typically handsome GNR structure in colourful brick, tile and wood.

Above Headlamp blazing, the final southbound 'Enterprise' of the day, the 20.10 out of Belfast on 1 August 2006, approaches Dundalk, the hills of County Armagh and the 575-metre Slieve Gullion, after which the preserved GNR 4-4-0 No 171 is named, on the horizon.

Below GNR 'QLG' 0-6-0 No 159 stands at Dundalk with a southbound goods on 6 August 1957. The driver seems to be taking a keen interest in what is happening beneath the footplate. There were 12 'QLGs', designed by Clifford and built between 1906 and 1911. *Norman Simmons*

Above No 85 *Merlin*, one of the handsome, sky-blue-painted Compound 4-4-0s designed by Glover in 1932, has steam to spare as it waits to depart with a Belfast to Dublin express on 5 August 1957. The first four carriages date from the late 1930s and '40s, the first being in the blue and cream livery introduced in 1950, chiefly for vehicles intended to work with railcars. The next three, and the much older vehicles at the rear of the train, are in mahogany. *Norman Simmons*

Below By 1961 ex-GNR steam engines were rapidly heading for oblivion and sad lines of them occupied several sidings at Dundalk Works. One was *Merlin*, but he was destined to avoid the breaker's torch and, after a lengthy overhaul by Harland & Wolff, was put in the care of the Railway Preservation Society of Ireland, with whom he has resumed his career on the main line. Revisiting his old haunts, he is seen here in the same location as the previous picture (which was taken from the footbridge), taking on water on a run from Belfast to Dublin in August 2002.

No 201 *Meath* stands at the north end of Dundalk station in May 1949. Barely a year old, there were five of these lightweight 'U' Class engines, which, together with the powerful, three-cylinder 'VS' Class engines, were the last 4-4-0s built anywhere in the world. Constructed by Beyer Peacock in Manchester, they were basically a 1915 design with a modernised cab, and were delivered in May 1948. The leading carriage is of interest, being a former LNWR Brake Composite, sent across the water by the LMS to replace vehicles destroyed in the bombing of Belfast, fitted with 5ft 3in bogies and much repanelled. *Kelland Collection*

Another carriage that started its career on the other side of the Irish Sea is IR No 3180. This is a Brake Generating Steam Van, originally BR Mark 1 No 34378, built in the 1950s, shipped over in 1972 and converted at Inchicore. One of the very last survivors of 22 such vehicles, it is seen at Dundalk in August 2002, at the rear of a train of Craven carriages forming a stopping train from Dublin Connolly.

Another member of the 1948 version of the 'U' Class, No 203 *Armagh*, stands at Dundalk with a two-coach train, the first one a clerestory, on 6 August 1957. *David Lawrence*

Above Memories of less happy times: the remains of No B201 have been dragged back to Dundalk after its freight train was hijacked by terrorists near the border in 1972, the crew sent packing and a bomb planted in the locomotive.

Below The 'Enterprise' pulls out of Dundalk on a very wet afternoon in August 1978, heading for Dublin. The locomotive is Northern Irish Railways No 101 *Eagle*. One of three 1,350hp Bo-Bo diesel-electric locomotives built especially for the 'Enterprise' service by BREL at Doncaster as sub-contactors to Hunslet in 1970, it is hauling a rake of BR Mark 2 carriages, built at the same time. There are many who consider these amongst the best-riding carriages ever to run in Ireland, smoother, perhaps, than the De Dietrich stock.

Above Dundalk is a handsome station, featuring multi-coloured brickwork and tiles, and plenty of ornate iron columns. Re-engined CIE Metro-Vickers Co-Co No 010 is seen arriving on 20 August 1978 with the 14.30 Dublin to 'Belfast Enterprise'.

Left The part the railway has played in the history of Dundalk has always been appreciated, and recently an exhibition has been set up in one of the waiting rooms on the long island platform, telling the story of the station and the railways that have served the town and the surrounding district.

Left Another reminder of Dundalk's railway history: two of the distinctive gates guarding the long-vanished rails near Jenkinstown on the shores of Dundalk Harbour, photographed in August 2006.

Above The GNR, out of financial necessity if for no other reason, was a great pioneer and long-time operator of motor buses, building its own at Dundalk between the 1930s and the 1950s. In this scene in the Square, Dundalk, Lancashire-built Leyland Tigers and Lions are gathered in about 1932. *Author's collection*

Below GNR railbus No 1, dating from 1934, was initially used on the Scarva branch, which had previously been closed. Converted from a Leyland Tiger road vehicle, it is seen here at Dundalk Works on 12 June 1958. It will be seen that the bus retains its pneumatic tyres. Two Dundalk engineers, Howden and Meredith, patented a device with the Dunlop tyre firm to enable this to work successfully. *John Langford*

In the years immediately after the Second World War the GNR operated AEC Regents between Dundalk and Newry, one of only three international cross-border double-deck routes anywhere in the world. One Regent has been preserved at the National Museum at Howth, and is seen here in the Museum grounds.

A 2004 Volvo of the Halpenny bus company in Newry in August 2006, operating the service to Dundalk. Bus Eireann also works this route.

Above This is the original GNR Dundalk Junction station, built on the curve that brought in trains from Castleblaney and Enniskillen. At the West Junction it connected with the line from Quay Street and Barrack Street stations. The line closed in 1960 but the station was still serving as a goods depot when this picture was taken in 1973.

Below The unique GNR crane tank, an 0-6-0T built by Hawthorn Leslie in 1928, is standing by Dundalk Square Crossing cabin, where the Dundalk, Newry & Greenore Railway crossed the GNR main line on the level. Beyond the crossing was Dundalk Works, where the crane tank was employed. *H. C. Casserley*

Above A Dundalk, Newry & Greenore Railway train passes over the GNR main line at Dundalk Square Crossing on 15 May 1950. This is the 10.25am train from Dundalk Junction station, out of which it has reversed to the West Junction, and is now continuing on its way to Quay Street, Barrack Street and all stations to Greenore. At this time many trains working Irish branch lines seemed to belong to a bygone era, but surely none could match the extraordinary apparition of what was to all intents and purposes a London & North Western Railway train of the late 19th century. The locomotive is a Webb saddle tank belonging to a class built between 1873 and 1898 and the carriages are Wolverton-built six-wheelers of the same period. Not only that, but all are in LNWR livery, something that had disappeared from England in the 1920s. *H. C. Casserley*

Below More than half a century later, in August 2006, a commuter train from Dublin, composed of a 29000 Class four-car DMU of IR, the first of which was delivered from Zaragoza, Spain, in 2001, with driving power car No 29103 leading, approaches Dundalk station. Surviving parts of the Works are on either side, with various Bus Eireann vehicles parked in the yard. The second carriage is passing the site of the Square Crossing.

Above GNR 2-4-2T No 94 runs around the 11.20am train from Greenore at Dundalk West Junction before pulling it into Dundalk Junction station on 14 April 1948. By this date many of the DN&GR trains were worked by these 'JT' Class engines, dating from 1895-1902, which had begun to appear on the line in 1933. *Author's collection*

Below Greenore station, seen here in 1949, wa substantially built of red brick and dated from the openin of the line in 1873. *Author's collection*

Above A Seatruck container ship, sailing from Warrenpoint, heads past Greenore for the bar and the open sea on its way to Heysham in July 2006. Until the 1920s Greenore was served by a regular service of cross-channel steamers to Holyhead. The service never really recovered from the appalling tragedy that befell the SS *Connemara* on the night of 3 November 1916. She was a twin-screw steamer, built for the LNWR by the well-known Dumbarton firm of Denny Brothers in 1897. The weather was dreadful, 'the wildest night he had experienced in 70 years', according to a local farmer, but the *Connemara* nevertheless set out for Holyhead at her regular time of 8pm with 51 passengers and a crew of 30, mostly Holyhead men. She was half a mile beyond the bar, a narrow channel 300 yards wide some 3 miles out of Greenore, when an incoming vessel, a cargo steamer from Garston, also entered the channel. The nearby Haulbowline lighthouse, seeing that there was a danger of collision in what was described as 'the sea churned into a fearful cauldron', fired warning rockets, but a huge gust of wind caught the *Retriever* and drove her into the side of the *Connemara*. Both sank, the passenger ship almost immediately, and although the rockets had attracted a number of people on land who had come to the water's edge, there was nothing they could do – except to pull in the single survivor. This was 21-year-old James Boyle, of the *Retriever*. Clinging to an upturned boat, he had somehow avoided being dashed on the rocks, and was dragged to safety by a farmer's son from Cranfield on the peninsula opposite Greenore. He was taken to his home at Warrenpoint, survived and lived on there until his death at the age of 72 in April 1967.

Above right By the late 1920s the DN&GR was losing money, and the passenger service from Greenore to Holyhead ended, although cattle traffic across the Irish Sea remained a steady source of income. The Second World War gave it a tremendous boost, as with so many branch lines in the north of Ireland, not the least of its increased business being related to goods that could be got in Eire but not in Northern Ireland. A Newry woman recalled, 'There were packed trainloads every day going to Greenore, and well packed bags on the way back. The customs officers mostly turned a blind eye. Tea was in very short supply in Eire and I can well remember certain "smart boys" ... swapping it for butter on the Eire shore.

Of course, if the customs man was waiting ... the only thing was to "drop it". Many a load of butter floated out to sea in Carlingford Lough.' With the return of peace, passengers and freight returned to the roads. Nationalisation in 1948 saw the DN&GR pass to the British Transport Commission. The GNR was offered it but declined, and the last train ran on 31 December 1951. More than 50 years later a surprising amount remains. This is Euston Street, Greenore, in the summer of 2006.

Below A reminder of how it all began and the LNWR links still to be seen in Greenore in August 2006.

On the line to Newry running beside Carlingford Lough, the closed station at Carlingford became the town's tourist office. A Bus Eireann coach working a service that replaced the trains is just leaving for Greenore in August 2006.

Webb 0-6-0ST No 6 *Holyhead* with its train of purple and off-white carriages, waits at Edward Street, Newry, with a Greenore train in about 1947. *Author's collection*

Drogheda, Navan and branches

Drogheda's first station was opened by the Dublin & Drogheda Railway in 1844, and was replaced in 1855 by the present one, built on a sharp curve leading to the Boyne Viaduct, which came into use on the same day, 5 April 1855. Designed by Sir John MacNeil, work began on the viaduct in June 1851 and it was completed nearly four years later. It consists of three spans, the central one 226 feet long, the two flanking ones each 141 feet. To look nearly 100 feet down on the town and the quays, usually with one or more ships loading or unloading, as one crosses high above is one of the great Irish railway visual experiences.

In 1850 the Dublin & Drogheda Railway opened a 17¼-mile-long line to Navan. The original station there, a terminus, survived until 1864, when it was replaced by the present one, on the opposite side of the viaduct completed in 1863. This station closed to passengers in 1958 but is still used by Irish Rail and may well revert to its original purpose one day. The line on to Kells, home of the most famous holy book in all of Ireland, 9½ miles from Navan, opened in 1853. The 12¾-mile extension to Oldcastle was completed ten years later. The Great Northern ceased running passenger trains between Drogheda and Oldcastle in April 1958, and all traffic on the former MGWR line from Clonsilla was ended by CIE in March 1961. However, the GNR line remained open for gypsum traffic thereafter, while the section from Navan West to Tara Mines, a half-mile-long branch, opened on 29 June 1977.

Navan was considered a sufficiently attractive proposition by both the GNR and the Dublin & Meath Railway, later absorbed by the MGWR, for the latter to open its 23¼-mile-long branch from Clonsilla, on its main line to the west, to Navan in 1862, 12 years after the GNR had reached the town. Clonsilla station itself had opened in 1847, closed in 1947, then – a sign of changing times – re-opened in 1981.

The MGWR's first terminus in Navan served until 1869, being replaced by Navan Junction, where the connection with the GNR was made. In 1872 the MGWR continued on for 15¼ miles to Kilmainham Wood, with a final 4¼ miles to Kingscourt opening in 1875. The entire line closed to passengers in 1947, but the line from Drogheda to Navan and Kingscourt, a quarter of a mile short of the terminus, is still open, although there is no traffic. With the Dublin suburbs expanding and commuters living further and further from the city, there is great pressure to re-open the line from Clonsilla to Navan, to which the Government has given outline agreement.

In October 1864 the Dublin & Meath Railway (later MGWR) opened the 12¼-mile-long branch from Kilmessan Junction, on the Clonsilla to Navan line, to Athboy, the section as far as Trim having opened on 15 December 1863. Closed to passengers in January 1947, and to goods traffic three months later, the branch lingered on in a sort of limbo, being served by livestock trains until 1953, then for wagon storage until January 1954. It was taken up in 1958.

Above right At Dromin Junction, between Dundalk and Drogheda, a branch line to Ardee diverged. This is the view on 5 June 1964, looking north. Dromin Junction station closed to regular passenger traffic in 1955. The next station to the south, Dunleer, 41¾ miles from Dublin Connolly, closed in 1976, re-opened in 1979, and closed again in 1984, but is the subject of a campaign to re-open it once again as the area along the coast becomes ever more popular with Dublin commuters. *John Langford collection*

Right The same day a former GSWR 'J15' 0-6-0, CIE No 183, travelled up the branch to Ardee with a special. Opened in 1896 and closed to regular passenger services in 1955, the branch eventually closed to goods in October 1975. *John Langford collection*

Left An August 1985 cab view from a train about to pass over the 508-foot-long, almost 100-foot-high Boyne Viaduct at Drogheda, completed in 1857.

Below The Belfast-bound 'Enterprise', composed of a rake of CIE railcars, crosses the Boyne Viaduct on 1 August 1959. *Frank Church*

Above GNR 'QG' No 154, a Clifford 0-6-0 dating from 1903-4, stands at Drogheda with a train from Oldcastle and Navan in the early 1950s. The train has been propelled back into the down platform having come off the branch. *Rev John Parker*

Below The Belfast-bound 8.30am 'Enterprise' from Dublin carefully negotiates the sharply curving down platform at Drogheda in 1973, hauled by re-engined Metro-Vickers Co-Co No A5R. The 31¼-mile-run from Connolly was at that time scheduled to take 34 minutes; today it is scheduled to take 4 minutes less. *Bernard C. Byrne*

Left IR General Motors Bo-Bos Nos 147 and 187, the former a 950hp loco dating from 1962, the latter a slightly more powerful 1,100hp loco delivered from La Grange, Illinois, in 1966, wait at Drogheda in July 2006. They are standing above the main Dublin to Belfast road at the beginning of the Navan branch.

Below left The RPSI train of preserved carriages is about to set off from Drogheda for Dublin on 1 September 1984 hauled by former NCC 2-6-4T No 4. The carriage nearest the camera is former GSWR 1st No 1142, built at Inchicore in 1921, next to it is former NCC North Atlantic Brake 3rd No 91 dating from 1936, and leading is the former GNR Directors' Saloon of 1911.

Bottom left In September 2003 Drogheda, always a busy railway town, took on much greater significance when a 42 million euro Commuter Railcar Service Depot was commissioned. Built on the site of the original terminus station of 1844, it serviced the entire IR fleet of 144 railcars. With three tracks within the depot, it employees a staff of 55, working shifts, much of the maintenance and overhaul being done at night so that the cars can leave by 6am ready to take up work. The depot was completed ahead of schedule and below cost, and one senses the pride of those who work there, 80 per cent of the workforce being from the Drogheda area.

Below A driver about to board a Dublin-bound DMU at Drogheda in August 2005.

Above Drogheda GNR shed in the early 1950s: 'QLG' No 164 of 1911 stands at the head of the line of three 0-6-0s. *Rev John Parker*

Below Re-engined Metro-Vickers Co-Co No 033 passes Beauparc, the long-closed last station before Navan on the branch from Drogheda, with the 10.05 Kingscourt-Drogheda goods train on 23 August 1974. *Aubrey Dale*

Left Navan signal box in August 2005, complete with fluorescent lighting but otherwise pure GNR and virtually identical to that at long-vanished Kells.

Left Kells had a standard GNR signal box, seen here looking back towards Drogheda on 3 June 1961. The line from Drogheda and Navan reached Kells in 1853. *R. M. Casserley*

Below An Irish Railway Record Society Special to Oldcastle on 3 June 1961 is seen at Kells, hauled by former GNR 'Q' Class 4-4-0 No 132 – note the CIE stencil on the buffer beam. The leading vehicle is one of the notorious four-wheel passenger guard 'tin vans' introduced by Bulleid and heartily disliked by the staff who had to ride in them. *Rev John Parker*

Above This is Oldcastle on 3 June 1961 during the visit of the RPSI special train. Sports jackets and grey flannels were more or less de rigueur for enthusiasts back in those days, the Swinging Sixties having not yet exerted its influence. The final part of this branch, from Kells to Oldcastle, was completed in 1863. Regular passenger traffic between Drogheda and Oldcastle ended in April 1958, and goods traffic in March 1961. *R. M. Casserley*

Below Clearly a number of the locals have turned out at Wilkenstown, on the Kingscourt branch, to witness the almost forgotten spectacle of a passenger train calling, in this case the RPSI special of 3 June 1961. For all that the station looks remarkably well cared for. *R. M. Casserley*

Top Nobber, the next station down the branch, was photographed on the same day. *R. M. Casserley*

Above The special has now reached Kilmainham Wood, the penultimate station on the Kingscourt branch. It is a wonder none of the participants were left behind, lost for ever amongst the encroaching undergrowth! *R. M. Casserley*

Left The terminus of the Kingscourt branch is just across the Louth border into Monaghan. The line was opened by the MGWR in 1875 and closed to passenger traffic in 1947. *R. M. Casserley*

Above This is Kilmessan Junction, on the Clonsilla to Navan branch, on 23 September 1957. The 6.30am goods from North Wall to Kingscourt is hauled by No 626, a 'J5' 0-6-0 built by Morton for the MGWR in the mid-1920s right at the end of its separate existence. *C. H. A. Townley*

Below The engine shed at Athboy, at the end of the branch from Kilmessan, was photographed in 1939. The branch-line engine taking water is No 552, one of 12 'J26' 0-6-0Ts built for the MGWR in 1890-3 by Sharp Stewart and Kitson. Despite being so widespread in England, Wales and Scotland, the 0-6-0T was relatively rare in Ireland, and the 'J26s' were among the most numerous. *W. A. Camwell*

Above An IRRS special, hauled by a former GNR 4-4-0, sits under the bridge at the approach to Dunboyne, the first station on the Clonsilla to Navan branch, on 3 March 1961. *Author's collection*

Below Clonsilla, once the junction for the Athlone line and likely to be so again, has had a somewhat chequered existence. Opened in 1847, it became the junction for Navan in 1862, was closed when the branch ceased to operate in November 1947, but came back to life with the resurgence in passenger traffic in November 1981. This is the scene looking towards Dublin in August 1985.

MALAHIDE AND HOWTH

Above Balbriggan, between Drogheda and Dublin, its station built right against the water's edge, is seen in 1986 with a Dublin Connolly to Drogheda stopping train approaching, hauled by GM Bo-Bo No 083.

Below GNR 'V' Class Compound 4-4-0 No 85 *Merlin* is seen near Malahide with an up Dublin-bound express on 28 May 1955. *Neil Sprinks*

Above Malahide has become an extremely popular place of residence over the last few years, particularly since the DART has been extended to it, bringing Connolly within 22 minutes, with trains every 10 minutes or so during peak travel hours. In this December 2004 picture the low winter sun highlights father and child, the overhead, and the awning of this beautifully cared-for, prize-winning station, still, despite modernisation, essentially as built by the GNR to the designs of W. H. Mullis in the 1890s.

Below This view of the former GNR main line, looking north, was taken from an aircraft landing at Dublin Airport in December 2003. In the middle distance is the causeway and viaduct carrying the line over the Malahide Estuary; Malahide station is just beyond the curve immediately before the estuary.

Former GNR No 131, a Clifford 'Q' 4-4-0 of 1899-1904, speeds through Howth Junction with a Dublin-bound train shortly after the dissolution of the GNR in 1958. The carriages are still in GNR livery. *Author's collection*

At Howth Junction in August 1976, push-pull unit No 6109, converted from a railcar set and propelled by a re-engined Metro-Vickers 'B' Class Bo-Bo, heads northwards with a stopping train for Drogheda.

Almost 30 years later, in August 2005, DART set No 8640 stands on the Howth branch at Howth Junction and will join the main line once the 'Enterprise', from which the picture was taken, has cleared the junction. The four-car EMU is an almost brand-new set built by Tokyu, Yokohama, Japan.

Howth, one of Ireland's principal fishing ports and, for a time, the port for mails between England and Ireland, was reached by a 3½-mile branch from Howth Junction on the Dublin to Drogheda line in 1847, a temporary terminus short of the town having opened a year earlier. The GNR ran electric trams from Sutton, the penultimate station on the branch, around the peninsula up to the heights overlooking Dublin Bay and back down to Howth from 1901 to 31 May 1959. Well patronised, particularly in summer, they were the last trams to operate in Ireland until the advent of the LUAS, and had they held on a while longer their popularity might have ensured their survival as part of the heritage movement, then only just beginning to make itself felt.

Above At Howth station on 27 April 1957, No 188, one of the 'T1' 4-4-2Ts of 1913, stands ready to depart for Amiens Street. The 'T1s', together with the slightly newer 'T2s', were the mainstay of Dublin suburban services until gradually replaced by diesel railcars. Beyond the fence is a tram, one of a fleet of ten introduced in 1901 to work the 5½-mile loop up to the summit of the Hill of Howth and back down to Sutton, the other station on the branch. *Hugh Davies*

Left One of the original DART EMUs, built by Link/Hofmann/Busch in 1983, at Howth in August 2006.

Above This is Sutton in December 2005, looking towards Howth Junction. Although the Hill of Howth was a popular destination for Dubliners in fine weather, the tramway on its own was losing more than £10,000 a year in its last years, although there are no figures to indicate its value as a feeder to the railway. It closed in 1959, but the tramway power house, seen beyond the signal box, survives as a factory. The signal box, now preserved, is no longer functional.

Below Three cars at the summit of the tramway on 9 June 1956. *Neil Sprinks*

Above Back on the main line, Raheny, 3¾ miles north-east of Amiens Street, is seen on 21 March 1954, with three-car set Nos 612/134/613 forming the 12.20pm service from Dublin. Introduced in 1950, these AEC-engined Park Royal-bodied railcars were based both on the GNR's experience with railcars in the 1930s and the GWR vehicles of that period. Today the surroundings have changed utterly, houses extending in all directions. *Neil Sprinks*

Below So impressed was CIE with the GNR cars that it ordered an almost identical fleet, initially for long-distance traffic but later used in the Dublin suburbs. These vehicles were eventually converted to push-pull units and two are seen here at Raheny in August 1976.

Midland Great Western lines

The Midland Great Western main line started from its highly impressive, if somewhat out-of-the-way, Egyptian-style terminus of Dublin Broadstone. Trains began to run as far as Enfield in June 1847, on to the Hill of Down in December of that year, to Mullingar in October 1848, and through to Athlone and Galway in August 1851. Broadstone was always the least busy of the Dublin termini, and in 1937 the Great Southern Railway closed it, the relatively few trains using it being diverted by way of Liffey Junction to Amiens Street and Westland Row, a much more convenient arrangement, bringing passengers from the west much closer to the city centre and enabling interchange with GNR and GSR suburban trains. Liffey Junction station, which had opened 1877, closed at the same time as Broadstone, although both remained in existence. Broadstone, of course, still does, being the headquarters of Bus Eireann. The engine shed remained in use at Broadstone into the early 1960s, and oil tankers continued to be brought down the single line from Liffey Junction for a while afterwards. Wagons destined for breaking up at Mullingar were stored in the sidings at Liffey Junction and the platforms were still in situ into the 1990s, but nothing remains now.

The Nesbitt Junction to Edenderry branch, 10¾ miles long, was opened by the MGWR in April 1877. It was, however, an early closure, to passengers in June 1931 and to goods in January 1935, but livestock traffic continued for another three decades, until April 1963.

Mullingar, 50¼ miles from Broadstone, became an important railway town, the junction for the main line due west to Athlone, Galway, Connemara and Mayo, and the north-west line to Sligo. The station, stone-built and quite impressive if a little bleak, is immediately beyond the divergence, with four through platform faces, two curving towards the west for up and down Athlone line trains and two curving away to the north, for the Sligo trains. Possibly rather over-provisioned, for services have never been exactly plentiful, there were extensive sidings, a locomotive shed and, beyond that, on the Athlone line, a depot for a track-laying system, designed by the MGWR's Chief Engineer, Arthur Breckland, in about 1920, which involved two rows of 500-foot-long impressive-looking gantries. Sadly it saw relatively little use and in later days became something of a pilgrimage centre for enthusiasts paying their last respects to time-expired carriages and wagons brought here from all over the CIE system for breaking up. There was also a hope that a preservation centre could be set up at Mullingar, but this project seems to have died in the last year or so. For many years the RPSI had use of the engine shed.

The line from Mullingar to Longford opened to passengers in November 1855 and precisely, and unusually, a year later to goods, the usual procedure being that goods traffic began before passenger. Seven years later trains commenced running between Dublin and Sligo. In the cash-strapped days of the late 1920s and early 1930s, after Southern Ireland gained its independence, most of the Midland main line was singled. There were protests, but in truth there was little inconvenience as traffic remained sparse.

In July 1856 at Inny Junction, 10¾ miles north of Mullingar, the MGWR opened a 23¼-mile branch to Cavan, where it connected with the GNR. It closed to passenger traffic in January 1947, and to goods traffic in January 1960.

The line from Mullingar to Athlone, 27¾ miles long, opened in 1851. Sparsely populated, particularly as the effects of the terrible Famine hit the area hard, there were only three intermediate stations between the two places, at Castletown, Streamstown and Moate, together with Newbrook, just outside Mullingar, which served the racecourse there and was closed early in GSR days. Castletown and Streamstown closed in 1963, and Moate in 1987 when all regular traffic ended, passenger trains for Athlone, Galway and Westport being diverted to the Portarlington route. This did not stop an estate agent in 2006 advertising 'a manageable property in Streamstown within commuting distance of Dublin for someone wishing to keep a few ponies'. There have been calls to re-instate passenger traffic, but this would involve considerable expense for the line has been signed out of use.

Streamstown was the junction for the 7¾-mile-long MGWR branch to the GSWR Portarlington-Athlone line at Clara, opened in April 1863. Regular traffic ended in January 1947, occasional specials ventured there a while longer, but total closure came in July 1965. The MGWR built its own station at Clara, which had been shut by the GSR in 1925. Another branch headed south-west from Clara, the 17¾-mile-long Clara & Banagher Railway, opened in 1894 and absorbed by the GSWR in 1895. It closed to passengers in February 1947 and completely in January 1963.

Above Carbury was the only intermediate station on the Edenderry branch from Nesbitt Junction, which was opened by the MGWR in 1877. It was an early closure to regular passenger traffic, which ceased in June 1939, and this was the view looking towards Edenderry on 9 June 1961. *Author's collection*

Left Edenderry station was photographed on the same day. Regular goods traffic ended a short while after passenger traffic, but livestock specials continued to be worked from here until April 1963. *Author's collection*

Above A 'J15' 0-6-0 stands at milepost 46, on the approaches to Mullingar, with an Irish Railway Record Society special on 2 September 1957. *David Lawrence*

Right This is Mullingar, looking past the sidings and locomotive shed towards the station in 1973. At this time Galway and Westport trains still passed this way, but would be diverted in 1985 by way of Portarlington. An elderly arc-roof GSWR carriage dating from the late 1890s is prominent.

Right Up and down Dublin-Sligo trains hauled by '071' locomotives and formed of BREL-built carriages pass at Mullingar in December 2004. The leading carriage of the Sligo-bound train is passing over the now disused line to Athlone.

Above The GSWR station at Athlone is seen on 12 June 1958. After the formation of the GSR in 1925 it became a goods depot, all passenger trains using the former MGWR station on the west bank of the Shannon. *A. E. Bennett*

Right '001' Class Co-Co No 020 stands at the former MGWR station at Athlone with the 08.20 Dublin to Westport via Mullingar train on 29 December 1978, seen from the doorway of the goods shed.

Below General Motors Bo-Bo No 183 hauls a mixed freight, with open wagons prominent – a feature of the railway scene now vanished – across the River Shannon at Athlone on a sunny but bitterly cold December morning in 1978.

Above With the diversion of Galway and Westport passenger trains away from the Mullingar to Athlone line, the Midland station at Athlone was closed and replaced by the extensively refurbished GSWR one, seen here shortly after re-opening as a passenger station in 1985.

Below No 083 stands with an up Galway train at the re-opened Athlone station in 1987.

Above A Dublin (Westland Row) to Galway train stands at Streamstown, between Mullingar and Athlone, the junction for Clara, on 20 April 1955. In early 1923, during the Civil War, there were several incidents of malicious damage at Streamstown in which a bridge was blown up, trains were deliberately run into each other and much damage was done, although there do not seem to have been any deaths. The station closed in 1963. *H. C. Casserley*

Below On 18 March 1963 former GSWR '101' Class 0-6-0 No 151 passes Horseleap, the one intermediate station on the Streamstown-Clara branch. *Author's collection*

At Clara on 23 June 1939 No 668, a former MGWR 'G2' 2-4-0 of 1893-8, heads a mixed train consisting of a former GSWR clerestory Brake Composite, complete with footboards, and a variety of wagons, passing the connecting platform on the former GSWR line bound for Athlone. *W. A. Camwell*

Above Smoke and steam drift across Clara on a sunny summer afternoon in about 1958 as a 'J18' 0-6-0 prepares to depart from the former MGWR station. *Brian Connell*

Below No 590, a former MGWR Atock 'J18' 0-6-0 of 1876-95 is about to draw forward into Clara station with the Banagher goods on 18 August 1959. *John Langford*

Great Southern & Western lines

Returning to Dublin, we move along the Quays from Broadstone and across the Liffey to Kingsbridge. Quite the grandest station in Ireland, at least when seen from the outside – it was nothing much to write home about inside – it was designed by Sancton Wood. A prolific designer of railway buildings, he did considerable work in Ireland and in East Anglia (the fine house he designed for himself near Ipswich recently came on the market). Kingsbridge was based on the design of an Italian palazzo, and is a riot, but a well-proportioned one, of Corinthian columns, balustrades, carved swags and urns, flanked by domed campaniles. Sadly the money ran out before the interior, and Sir John McNeil's trainshed, could be completed. The roof was low, not like the soaring arches of a St Pancras, Paddington or even Westland Row, giving a dark, gloomy feel. For more than 100 years Kingsbridge station consisted of just two main platforms with four sidings between them, as in many of the very earliest English termini. Traffic in the latter soon meant extensive rebuilding, but it is a sign of how sparse business was in and out of Kingsbridge, not helped by the complete absence of any commuter business, that this situation existed for more than a century, with the exception of a relatively short bay platform known as the 'military platform', installed chiefly to serve the British Army at the Curragh.

Kingsbridge was completed for the Great Southern & Western Railway in 1848 and would become the headquarters of the country's largest railway system, extending to more than 1,100 track miles. The first GSWR train had actually run some three years earlier when, in June 1845, directors and friends travelled over a short section of track near Sallins, while 4 August 1846 saw the first public trains running between Dublin and Carlow. Carlow, 56 miles from Dublin, was actually on the line to Kilkenny, which left the main line to Cork at Cherryville Junction, 32½ miles from Dublin. The continuation of the line to Cork opened in various stages, to Portlaoise in June 1847, to Ballybrophy in September of that year, and across the Munster border to Thurles in March 1848. October 1849 saw the first train leave Cork for Dublin. Initially there were just two through trains in each direction: the Mail, which took 7 hours, and another, stopping everywhere and the only one to carry 3rd Class passengers, taking 12 hours.

Sallins, 17¾ miles from Kingsbridge, was the site of the first branch from the GSWR main line. Opened in June 1885, it wended its way more or less due south for 34¾ miles through Counties Kildare, Wicklow and Carlow to Tullow. Colbinstown and Baltinglass were temporary termini, Tullow, its ultimate destination, being reached in June 1886. Passenger services ended in January 1947 and goods two months later, while cattle specials continued to struggle on until finally surrendering to the ever-encroaching weeds and undergrowth in April 1959.

At Curragh, 27½ miles from Kingsbridge, a half-mile-long branch to serve the racecourse and the large military camp on this wide, flat, grassy expanse was opened in 1856. This had a rather longer existence than most such specialised branches, or perhaps more accurately lengthy sidings, not being taken out of use until 1977.

Portarlington, 41¾ miles from Kingsbridge, has been a junction since 1854 and, unlike many, has become more important in recent times. Designed by Sancton Wood, the station was an impressive one, although it was not quite ready when trains began to run from Dublin in June 1847. It became a junction when the GSWR opened the 15¾-mile-long line to Tullamore in 1854, extending this another 23½ miles to Athlone five years later. It built its own station there, just before the junction with the MGWR and the River Shannon Bridge; being a place of considerable importance, the GSWR saw no reason why its rival should have a monopoly of the town's traffic. Eventually, long after both companies had been consigned to history, the Galway and Westport line trains were, as we have seen, in 1973 diverted from the MGWR route via Mullingar to the Portarlington one, the MGWR station on the west bank of the Shannon was closed, and the GSWR one, which had been closed to passengers and used solely for goods since 1925, once again, after refurbishing, became a passenger station.

As a local historian notes, 'This has made Portarlington into a busy interchange for student travel on Friday and Sunday evenings from October to May, with numbers far exceeding the capacity of the waiting rooms.' Twenty years earlier the Rev R. B. Bantry White recalled in the Journal of the Irish Railway Record Society the scene at Portarlington 30 years before that:

> 'The platforms are very low, as they were until the early 1970s. The limestone Gothic buildings shine in the sun… The parcels office is full of bundles of newspapers and parcels awaiting collection, while outside stands a station barrow on which some boxes of herrings drip smelly water on this hot day; all the older luggage vans were pickled by 50 years of weekly fishwater… Nearby is a notice bearing the name of Mr Ormsby, once the GSWR's secretary, which threatens a fine of Not More Than 40 Shillings for each offence of trespass… Another porter is setting off on his once-weekly walk to each of the three Distant signals, with the oil lamps that he has filled and trimmed in the lamp room on the up platform. Further down, behind the platform, is heard the thudding of red Guinness barrels, many different sizes, being unloaded from an HB [ie a soft-topped goods and cattle wagon]. At the end of the platform, in the short siding, stands an ancient MGWR travelling crane with its runner, both now very crooked on their springs.'

Portlaoise, originally Maryborough, 51 miles from Kingsbridge, was at one time served by a quite complicated network of lines. Immediately after parting company with the Cork main line, trains on their way to Kilkenny encountered Conniberry Junction. This threw off a branch line to Mountmellick, a small town some 7 miles due north, to reach which it had to dive under the main line. The reason for this curious arrangement was that it was intended to be part of a through route from Waterford and Kilkenny to Mullingar. Equally curious is the fact that it was partly financed by the English Great Western Railway. But then both the GWR and the LNWR were always sticking their fingers into the Irish pie, hoping to pull out a plum and at the same time thwart the other. Sometimes they succeeded, but over the years they must have lost more money than they ever made. The branch was opened by the Waterford & Central Ireland Railway in 1885 and was closed to passengers by CIE in 1947, and to freight in 1963.

Ballybrophy, 66½ miles from Dublin, was another location where a branch line took off in the wrong direction, so to speak – ie trains from Dublin had to reverse to gain it. Ballybrophy has rejoiced in a number of names over the years. It started out in 1847 as Borris & Roscrea and after ten years became Roscrea & Parsonstown Junction before, in 1870, assuming its present title. The reason for the addition of 'Junction' change was the logical enough one that in 1857 it had indeed become the junction for Roscrea when a 10-mile line belonging to the GSWR to that town was completed. Six years later it was extended 19½ miles to Nenagh, and a year later a further 13 miles to Birdhill. Here it met up with the Limerick & Castleconnell Railway's 4¼-mile-long line from Castleconnell, which had opened in 1860. This was a continuation of the line from Killonan Junction that had reached Castleconnell, 5½ miles distant, in 1858. From Killonan access was gained to Limerick, something over 4 miles away, by the metals of the Waterford & Limerick Railway, which had opened in 1848. Thus through trains were now able to run from Ballybrophy via Nenagh to Limerick, which they continue to do to this day.

At Roscrea a 11¾-mile branch was completed by the Roscrea & Parsonstown Railway (Birr was Parsonstown until 1900) in March 1858. It closed to all traffic in January

1963. What was possibly the shortest-lived public steam railway in Ireland – apart from that to Magilligan Point, which came and went within 12 months – linked Parsonstown with the River Shannon at Portumna Bridge. Less than a mile of it was actually in Leinster, the rest heading west through County Tipperary. It was worked from the outset by the GSWR, which had an agreement to do so for ten years, and when that time was up the company, seeing no possibility of covering its expenses, took itself off – end of railway.

Swinging southwards at Cherryville Junction and heading down the Carlow line, Athy, 12¼ miles on, used to be the junction for a rather unusual branch line. Opened in September 1918 and financed by the British government, it served two collieries at Wolfhill, namely Gracehill and Modubeagh. In 1921 the Irish Free State government took over the collieries and the GSWR the railways serving them, and there were some fascinating and very well-informed exchanges in the Dail at the time concerning their viability. The newly established Free State was hardly born with a silver spoon in its mouth, and if it could make use of its own natural resources rather than having to import coal from Britain then this was clearly highly desirable. There was coal up at Arigna, served by the Cavan & Leitrim narrow gauge lines, and the only other significant seam of coal was down in Counties Kilkenny and Laois. However, as one TD pointed out, the quality varied considerably, that at Wolfhill being much lower than that at Deerpark. Another TD argued that Wolfhill would be a lot more successful if there was sufficient cutting equipment, if enough skilled miners could be found, and if those could then be kept continuously employed rather than taking themselves off to better-paid work in Scotland whenever things got slack at Wolfhill. In the event the collieries at Wolfhill struggled on until 1929 when they and the railway closed down, being outlived by Deerpark by more than 30 years. The initial 4½ miles, to the beet siding at Ballylinan, remained in use until April 1963.

The Deerpark line left the Kilkenny-Portlaoise line at Castlecomer Junction, 3¾ miles north of Kilkenny, and was some 9¾ miles long. A series of overhead cable cars brought the coal from the various pits to the railhead and, despite the Free State's own requirements, much of the coal was actually exported, being shipped from Dublin to Britain. A local historian, Tom Lyng, noted that enquiries for the coal were received from as far away as Cairo, Sao Paulo and Stockholm, although it is not clear whether it actually got that far. Well into the 1950s three trains were needed daily. Crumbling remains of the colliery buildings can still be seen.

Passenger traffic to and from Castlecomer operated between 1921 and 1931 but excursions continued almost until the branch closed in 1963. One elderly Castlecomer resident, interviewed by Katherine Blake in 2005, recalled a journey in 1947:

> 'We went to Tramore and it was my first time at the seaside. I will never forget the excitement. One hundred and thirty people got the train from Castlecomer to Kilkenny, which took 40 minutes, and then we changed to the Waterford train. When we arrived in Waterford we had to get to the other side of the city to catch the Tramore train… We got to Tramore at 4 o'clock that afternoon,' she says, laughing at the memories. 'I remember my mother saying to me, "Well, there's the sea," but it was an overcast day and the sea and the sky were the same colour and all I could see was sky and I started crying. But we all went off down to the beach and, of course, the sea and the sand was so soft. It was lovely. It was a great day.'

One is a little puzzled as to why the branch-line train, which must have been a special, as it was 16 years on from the end of scheduled services, only took them as far as Kilkenny and why they set out so late in the day; one also wonders how they got back, but there it is. Your author's first visit to Tramore, long after the railway, which was isolated from the rest of the Irish system, had closed, was to see his sons' former head teacher, Sister Rosarii of the Sisters of Mercy, who had moved from England to Waterford, and who took us down to Tramore to see the holiday house that the nuns had there. Unlike that day in 1947 it was a glorious sunny one and Tramore looked a delightful place. When the branch closed in 1961 CIE put on as a replacement three AEC Regent double-deck buses with extra luggage space, one of which has been preserved, but as we have now strayed into Munster you can ignore those last pieces of information if you wish...

Continuing south through Carlow, 55¾ miles from Kingsbridge, the Irish South Eastern Railway opened the line to Bagenalstown, now called Muine Bheag, 66 miles from Dublin. The line carried on a further 24 miles through Borris and Ballywilliam to Palace East, where it connected with the Dublin & South Eastern Railway line from Waterford to Macmine Junction and Wexford. It opened in sections, to Borris in December 1858, to Ballywilliam in March 1862, and was completed in October 1870. There was nothing particularly difficult about the terrain, apart from the construction of the Borris Viaduct. This and the problems of raising sufficient capital to complete a railway, which passed through no large centres of population, accounted for the slow progress.

Meanwhile at Bagenalstown a second line owned by the Irish South Eastern headed

Looking back from the cab of a General Motors 'B' Class Bo-Bo in charge of a Cork to Dublin train near Adamstown in July 1973.

As the Dublin suburbs continue to grow, so huge investment is being put into the railways and the LUAS tram system to cope with the ever-increasing demand for up-to-date public transport. Adamstown, 7½ miles and 19 minutes by train from Heuston, and 15 minutes from Sallins, has been designed from the outset as a complete community, with shops, schools, churches, etc, being built at the same time as houses and, crucially, a railway station. On 29 March 2008 DMU No 29102, forming the 12.26 Newbridge to Heuston service, approaches the newly opened station at exactly the same location as the 1973 picture. Adamstown has been provided with four platforms, although only Nos 1 and 2 had tracks when this picture was taken, and work was in progress on building the two additional tracks to serve platforms 3 and 4.

south-westwards to Kilkenny, 14¾ miles distant, and was completed in 1850. Here it met the two-year-old line of the Waterford & Kilkenny Railway, heading up from Thomastown. This was 10¾ miles from Kilkenny, and passengers between Dublin and Waterford had to either wait two years for the viaduct over the River Nore to be completed, or make other arrangements to cross the river and continue by road. The viaduct, with a span of 212 feet, was ready for traffic in 1850. The railway continued on from Jerpoint Hill (which I always think sounds like the site of a battle in the American Civil War), on the southern bank, in 1853. It was opened for traffic in May of that year as far as Dunkitt, 16½ miles from Jerpoint Hill and within sigh of Waterford, 2 miles away. Sixteen month: later the Waterford & Limerick Railway completed its long cross-country line as far a Dunkitt, which it had begun in 1848, and in September 1854 trains from Dublin and Limerick finally reached Waterford proper This first station was called Waterfor (Newrath). Ten years later the present station a few hundred yards further on and the known as Waterford North, opened. Th Waterford & Kilkenny Railway briefly used terminus at Newrath Commons, betwee October 1867 and April 1868. In 196 Waterford North was renamed Waterfor Plunkett.

Above Another Cork to Dublin express passes Sallins in August 1975. The locomotive, No 011, is one of the 'A' Class re-engined in February 1971 by General Motors and upgraded to 1,325hp, most importantly thereby being rendered vastly more reliable. It this form it served for a further 22 years, being withdrawn and broken up at Inchicore in late 1995.

Right Two 29000 Class DMUs, working the Heuston-Kildare stopping service in August 2006, pass at the Dublin end of Sallins station, where No 011 was pictured 31 years earlier.

When it opened in 1846, Sallins station was known as Sallins & Naas, but it lost the second half of its title when the Tullow branch opened in 1885 and Naas station proper was built. CIE closed Sallins station in 1963, but IR re-opened it in May 1994, when it reverted to its original title.

The handsome station buildings are boarded up but the station itself, now very much within the Dublin commuter area, is busier than ever. A train of Mark 2 stock calls early on an August morning in 2006 and will reach Dublin Heuston 26 minutes later, whence its passengers can alight and board a LUAS tram to whisk them into the commercial heart of the city.

At one time Sallins was where elderly carriages were set aside before their very last journey to the breakers' yard at Mullingar. One carriage – the only one? – that survived the journey was No 861, the 12-wheel Corridor Brake Composite built at Inchicore by the GSWR in 1906 for the boat trains that were inaugurated with the opening of the Rosslare to Cork line. Latterly painted black and used on the Inchicore Works train, it was rescued at the last minute by the RPSI and is seen here at Sallins in 1972. Its arc-roof companion, from the top of which this picture was taken, was less fortunate; the view is looking towards No 861's clerestory, and the signal box at the south end of the station that once controlled the turn-out for the Tullow branch.

Above An REC/IRRS special stands on the Tullow branch at Sallins on 21 September 1957. All regular services had finished by the end of March 1947, but livestock specials continued to run until April 1959. The track is just about visible in the grass. *John Langford*

Below An animated scene at Naas, the first station on the Tullow branch, 2¼ miles from Sallins. The occasion is probably a special, possibly the one featured in the previous picture. *IRRS collection*

Above The special of 21 September 1957 was hauled by former GSWR Aspinall-designed 'D14' Class 4-4-0 No 64 of 1885-95, which is seen here being turned on the Tullow turntable. *L. A. Dench*

Below On the same day No 64 is now in the station at Tullow, where the overall roof is still intact. The track was clearly not designed for high-speed travel! *Hugh Davies*

Above General Motors Bo-Bo No B166 heads south, having negotiated Cherryville Junction and gained the single-track line to Kilkenny and Waterford with a North Wall-Waterford freight in August 1973.

Right The driver of a GM 'B141' Class locomotive on the Cork to Dublin main line between Cherryville Junction and Kildare in about 1970.

Below No B135, one of the original single-ended 'B' Class 950hp General Motors Bo-Bos of 1960, heads west with a Limerick train in August 1973. The distinctive Cherryville Junction signal box is visible in the distance.

Above No 083 speeds westwards with the evening Dublin-Cork Mail near Cherryville Junction in August 1985.

Below Cherryville today: No 071 speeds into the setting sun with an evening Dublin-Cork train in August 2000.

Above The handsome GSWR-designed station buildings at Athy, dating from 1846, were photographed on 9 July 1960. *H. C. Casserley*

Right This is Athy looking north towards Cherryville Junction on the same date. It will be seen that the buildings are above platform level and are reached by a flight of steps, past an ornate stone balustrade. *H. C. Casserley*

Right Passengers, having alighted from the 13.20 Waterford to Dublin train in August 2002, head past the balustrade towards the steps. A coat of dark green paint has been applied in the intervening 42 years, and semaphore signals are still in place.

Above The Wolfhill branch, which diverged from the Cherryville-Kilkenny line south of Athy, is seen on 14 June 1958. At that date most of the branch, to two collieries opened in 1918 and closed in 1929, had long since disappeared, but beet traffic was still carried on part of it, while there was also a railway-served asbestos factory. *John Langford*

Below Carlow, seen on 10 June 1962 looking south towards Bagenalstown (today called Muine Bheag), was another fine GSWR station, dating from 1846. There was clearly no shortage of chimneys or pinnacles back then. The footbridge is rather unusual, having stone steps leading to a covered crossing of the tracks. *John Langford*

• GREAT SOUTHERN & WESTERN LINES •

Above The plug doors of the BREL-built air-conditioned carriages are open as the 13.20 service from Waterford calls at Carlow in August 2002.

Below In August 2002 the 15.00 service from Dublin Heuston arrives at Carlow at 16.10 behind IR Co-Co No 071 while a '201' Co-Co waits for the road with the 16.13 departure, which had arrived 2 minutes early.

Above Muine Bheag, originally Bagenalstown, boasted yet another range of ornate GSWR station buildings, which flourished in this part of Leinster. In this September 1973 picture, looking north, a 'J15'-hauled RPSI special is in the down platform. The leading carriage is a contemporary CIE one, next No 88, a former GNR tea car of 1936 and, nearest the camera, the famous No 861, the GSWR-built 12-wheel Brake Composite. *R. M. Casserley*

Below Across on the opposite platform from the previous picture, an IR '201' Class Co-Co is about to set off for Dublin in August 2002.

Above An unusual visitor to Kilkenny on 17 August 1960 is former GNR 'U' Class 4-4-0 No 197 *Lough Neagh*, seen being turned on the turntable. The roof of the station can just be seen behind No 197's tender. *John Langford*

Right A Waterford-Dublin train stands clear of the rather dilapidated-looking, redundant roof of Kilkenny station in August 2004. The line used to continue on through the station to Abbeyleix and Portlaoise, some Dublin trains dividing here, but since the beginning of 1963 all trains reverse and head for Dublin by way of Muine Bheag.

Right The 15.38 train is about to depart from Kilkenny for Dublin in August 2004. It has a 10-minute wait here while the locomotive, a '201' Class, runs round. Another '201' is waiting to enter the goods yard where a Guinness wagon can be glimpsed.

Above At Deerpark Siding on 17 August 1960 No 197 *Lough Neagh* is about to return down the branch with its RPSI special to Castlecomer and the junction with the Kilkenny-Portlaoise line. The branch, regular passenger traffic having long gone, closed completely on New Year's Day 1963. *John Langford*

Left This is the attractive approach to the attractive-looking Abbeyleix station on 6 June 1961, complete with horse, cart, carter and beer barrels, with enthusiasts from a special lurking in the background. *R. M. Casserley*

Left The RPSI special stands at the platform at Abbeyleix on the same day. The station remained in service for 98 years, from 1865 to 1963. *R. M. Casserley*

Above '101' Class 0-6-0 No 110 pauses at Portarlington with a local goods train on 16 May 1954. Examples of the rather elegant, standard GSWR iron footbridge can still be found at various locations on the IR system. *C. H. A. Townley*

Below Despite being designed by Atock for the MGWR, by the date of this picture, 16 June 1954, 'J18' 0-6-0 No 587 is able to do an excellent impersonation of a '101' with its GSWR-type boiler and cab. It is about to set off from Portarlington with the 6.55pm train to Athlone, which consists of three former GSWR corridor carriages, the first one elliptical-roofed, the next two with the older arc roof, then a six-wheel van, and two modern steel-bodied CIE carriages bringing up the rear. *C. H. A. Townley*

Left A train of the latest Spanish-built CAF carriages with Driving Brake Generator Van No 2003 leading, approaches Portarlington in October 2005, passing over the junction with the line from Athlone. *Danny Hathaway*

Left '071' Class No 075 stands at Portarlington with a train from Limerick in October 2005. *Danny Hathaway*

Below Intended by the Central Ireland Railway to be a passing place on a line to Mullingar, its ambitions far outstretched its finances and Mountmellick was as far as this branch got from Conniberry Junction on the Dublin to Kilkenny line. Opened in 1885, it closed to all regular traffic in January 1947; beet specials ran for another 16, and this enthusiasts' special called on 6 June 1961. *H. C. Casserley*

The 10.15am stopping train to Limerick Junction is about to set off from Ballybrophy behind 'D2' Class 4-4-0 No 322 on 24 April 1953. The featherweight load of two elderly GSWR carriages, one arc-roofed, one slightly more modern with an elliptical roof, is hardly a taxing load for the big 6ft 7in Coey locomotive, dating from 1904-06 and once assigned to the principal Dublin to Cork expresses. Today three of the five stations then open between Ballybrophy and Limerick Junction are closed. *H. C. Casserley*

In August 1957 No 307, one of the similar 'D12' 4-4-0s of 1902, its original taper boiler, like that of No 322, long ago having been replaced by a parallel one, waits at Ballybrophy with a two-coach train for Clonmel, which will turn off the main line at Thurles Junction and head off down the branch – first stop the intriguingly named Horse and Jockey – to its destination on the Waterford-Limerick Junction line. The Thurles to Clonmel branch closed to passengers in 1963, and to goods four years later. *C. H. A. Townley*

Left GM '071' Class Co-Co No 078 speeds through Ballybrophy with a Cork-bound train of air-conditioned BREL Mark 3 carriages in August 2001.

Right The somewhat basic Brosna Halt, the only intermediate station – well, stop – on the Birr branch from Roscrea, is seen on 24 April 1953. The branch closed on the first day of 1963. *H. C. Casserley*

Below The branch terminus at Birr was photographed on the same day, looking back towards Roscrea and Ballybrophy. The locomotive is No 295, a former GSWR Kitson 'E2' 2-4-2T of 1895, and the carriages are 21M and 38M, the suffix indicating their MGWR origin. *H. C. Casserley*

Waterford

With the completion by the Dublin, Wicklow & Wexford Railway of its New Ross and Macmine Junction line, the city of Waterford could boast three more or less direct routes to Dublin, which was more than other provincial city could muster, fittingly perhaps for Ireland's oldest city. In all Waterford was served by a grand total of six lines – seven really, if we count the Carlow and Abbeyleix routes as separate. However, relations between the various companies, as we shall see, were not always what one would have wished.

Following the opening of the Carlow route in 1850, the Kilkenny Junction Railway completed a 28¼-mile branch from Portlaoise, or Maryborough as it then was (51 miles from Kingsbridge), in May 1867. The 18¾-mile section between Abbeyleix and Kilkenny opened in March 1865. The line just failed to reach its centenary, being closed by CIE on the first day of 1963. Some Bord na Mona traffic was carried on a short section at the Portlaoise end after this, and the 1¼ miles of track are still in place but out of use.

As the GSWR had in the early days no direct route wholly owned by itself between Dublin and Waterford, it tried to persuade passengers to travel a highly roundabout one by way of Limerick Junction. Mr Fletcher, the local manager of the Waterford & Kilkenny Railway, announced on 2 August 1854 that arrangements had been completed for through trains between Waterford and Dublin, but he was either over-optimistic or misled, for nothing of the sort happened. Perhaps the GSWR had been put off co-operating with a railway company that the *Irish Railway Gazette* said had been 'driven almost to bankruptcy'. Much of the fault lay outside Ireland, for most of the shareholders, who did not seem to have a great deal of business sense, were Bristol men, the board met in London, and all seemed to be singularly out of touch with what was happening across the water. It was no wonder that the company was accused of 'the grossest mismanagement'. The desperate shareholders dismissed the board and the new one tried to sell the railway, but no-one was foolish enough to come forward. Disputes continued with its neighbours; on 1 October 1867 the Waterford & Limerick refused to let the morning train to Kilkenny depart from its Newrath station, violence was threatened, the W&K erected its own very temporary station a little way distant, and the episode became known as the Battle of Newrath. Eventually the two companies came together, the Waterford & Limerick taking over working of the Waterford & Kilkenny in 1861. Renamed the Waterford & Central Ireland Railway in July 1868, it was absorbed by the GSWR in July 1900.

In the early days the journey between Waterford and Dublin was painfully slow. Passengers had to change at Kilkenny and the overall time was 5 hours. That is if you had a 1st or 2nd Class ticket. As Kevin Murray recalls, the GSWR cared so little for 3rd Class passengers that they sometimes had to stay overnight in Kilkenny, the one train with 3rd Class carriages leaving for Dublin 3 hours before the train from Waterford arrived. It was only with the GSWR take-over in 1900 that through carriages were put on. The journey in the early years of the 20th century took 3 hours 15 minutes. Trains divided at Kilkenny and you could continue on to Dublin either via Portlaoise or Carlow.

Above Waterford & Central Ireland Railway 2-4-0 No 3 is at the west end of Waterford station on 5 August 1900. Built by Stothert, Slaughter & Co in 1852, it was taken into GSWR stock in 1900 but scrapped shortly afterwards. *LCGB, Ken Nunn Collection*

Below Two General Motors 950hp Bo-Bos were photographed a few hundred yards beyond the previous location, alongside the River Suir, in August 1976.

Above Two Park Royal/AEC railcars call at New Ross in about 1955. Unfortunately the introduction of such modern, comfortable vehicles was not able to ensure the survival of passenger services here. *Rev John Parker*

Below A General Motors Bo-Bo shunts the daily goods from Waterford at New Ross in August 1976.

Below right In August 2005 it was still just possible to see where the track passed over the level crossing at the south end of New Ross station, but the replica sailing ship, the *Dunbrody*, tied up on the opposite bank of the river, makes a far more attractive picture. It was launched in 2001 by Bertie Ahern, An Taoiseach, and Mrs Jean Kennedy Smith, the US Ambassador to Ireland and sister of the late President, John F. Kennedy; on his visit to Ireland JFK had stood on the quayside at New Ross and recalled that his great-grandparents had left during the Great Famine for America in 1849. The *Dunbrody* is a full-size replica of the original emigrant ship built for the Graves family of New Ross in 1845.

Above Barrow Bridge, between New Ross and Palace East, was still in place in August 2005, although it was 42 years since a train had last crossed it.

Below Goresbridge was the first station on the Muine Bheag (Bagenalstown)-Palace East branch, and is seen here on 9 July 1960, complete with Morris Minor saloon and now-preserved 'J15' No 184. The less than perfect condition of the lightly laid track says much about CIE's expectations of the line's survival. It closed completely on 1 April 1963. *R. M. Casserley*

Above 'J15' No 187 approaches Palace East with a goods train from the Carlow line in about 1957. Palace East gets its intriguing name from the seat of King Brandubh, who ruled Leinster in about 590 AD; the remains of his palace can still be seen from the air. Later, Oliver Cromwell caused the locals to deposit their valuables in a well as he approached – sadly, the well has never been found... Unfortunately there's no chance of taking the train to start digging, for the last passenger service left in March 1963. *David Lawrence*

Below This is Palace East station looking west on 9 July 1960. *R. M. Casserley*

Above A 'J15' passes Palace East with the afternoon train to Waterford on 26 April, 1955. *Author's collection*

Below The morning Dublin to Rosslare train, hauled by 'D4' 4-4-0 No 335, arrives at Macmine Junction on 6 April 1953. The New Ross line branches off to the left beyond the water tank. *A. W. Burges*

ROSSLARE TO DUBLIN

We now make our way from Waterford to Rosslare, then up the east coast back to Dublin. The line between Dublin and Rosslare was completed in June 1882 and its history is a highly complicated one, a number of companies being involved in its construction and operation. The first section, from Westland Row to Kingstown (or Dunleary, an anglicised spelling of Dun Laoghaire) was the very first railway in the country and opened in 1834. We will look at this in rather more detail later. The next section, to Dalkey, reached in 1844, involved a certain Isambard Kingdom Brunel, but did not initially involve steam locomotives. Dalkey was then a village outside, but within walking distance of, Dublin. From there, along the most spectacular bit of railway in all Ireland, to the seaside resort of Bray, 13¼ miles from Dublin, the line was opened by the Dublin, Wicklow & Wexford Railway (DWWR) in July 1854. At Shanganagh, 1½ miles short of Bray, another line from the capital came in, from Harcourt Street. This opened in 1876 and was actually considered the main line, although it gradually came to be overshadowed by the coastal route and closed in 1959 – only to be re-opened as the wonderful LUAS, but that's another story.

Beyond Bray the line climbs again, around the cliffs overlooking the Irish Sea, which over the years has caused numerous problems and re-alignments. It reached Wicklow Town, 29¾ miles from Dublin, in October 1855. Rathdrum (37¾ miles) was reached in August 1861, Avoca (or Ovoca as it then was, 44¼ miles) in July 1863, Enniscorthy (79 miles) in November of that year, Wexford (93¾ miles from Dublin) in August 1872, and finally Rosslare Harbour (113½ miles from the capital) in June 1882.

The line from Wexford South to Rosslare Strand and Rosslare Pier rapidly fell on hard times and closed, except for the occasional cattle special, in May 1889. However, such a potentially strategically important link could not be allowed to disappear, and the Waterford & Wexford Railway was taken over by a new concern, the Fishguard & Rosslare Railways & Harbours Company, in 1894. Jointly owned by the Great Southern & Western Railway and the Great Western Railway, it carried considerable financial clout and the section between Wexford and Kilrane on Rosslare or South Bay re-opened on August 1894, and that to Rosslare Pier the following year.

The Dublin to Rosslare line could boast only two branch lines, one of the reasons for this paucity being the high hills and mountains immediately to the west of the line for much of its route, another the deeply rural character of the south-east. At Woodenbridge, 46¼ miles from Dublin, the DWWR opened the 16¾-mile-long branch to Shillelagh in May 1865. Trains ceased to run, except for the 4½ miles to Aughrim, in April 1944. This was supposed to be a temporary closure – something that happened all over the country at that time – because of the shortage of fuel, but passenger trains, except for the occasional special, never ran again. Goods train ran as far as Aughrim until May 1953. Considering that the branch was so long gone, I was surprised to discover, in the summer of 2005, how much remained at Shillelagh, a remote but beautiful spot in a deep valley. The station, still with its platform, is now a rather splendid home, whilst the goods shed serves as changing rooms for the GAA.

Macmine was one of those rural junction stations that served as an interchange but was far from any community and as such, when it ceased to be a junction, it ceased to serve any purpose and vanished. I take a certain delight in having actually arrived at it in a scheduled steam train, one of only two steam-hauled journeys I managed in pre-preservation days in Ireland. At 84¾ miles from Dublin, it was part of a through route from Waterford to Dublin, completed by the DWWR in 1904.

The line from Wexford to Rosslare Pier was opened by the Waterford & Wexford Railway, later absorbed into what would become the Dublin & South Eastern Railway. The Harbour Pier extension was part of the ambitious scheme completed in August 1906 that, with much input from the Great Western Railway, brought into existence the Fishguard

& Rosslare Railways & Harbours Company. The present terminus of Rosslare Europort, a quarter of a mile landward, dates from September 1989, although from that date until May 1996 it was still known as Rosslare Pier. The 1906 tracks were used for stabling stock but are now gone.

At the north end of Rosslare Strand station, slightly under 4 miles from Rosslare Europort, the Waterford and Dublin lines diverge. The Waterford line, completed in 1906, heads westwards through the flat, damp lands of south Wexford by way of Bridgetown, Wellington Bridge, Ballycullane and Campile, across the Barrow by a bridge of 14 spans (one of them opening), which, at 2,131 feet, is the longest in Ireland, into County Kilkenny, and through the 217-yard-long Snow Hill Tunnel.

Above The 16.25 Waterford to Rosslare Harbour train, hauled by GM Bo-Bo No 186, comes off the longest bridge in the country, the 14-span, 2,131-foot-long Barrow Bridge, 5½ miles east of Waterford, in August 1976.

Right The 07.00 service from Rosslare Europort, formed by DMU No 2710, heads through the Barrow Bridge on its way to Waterford on 25 July 2007.

Rosslare to Dublin

Above The 18.30 Rosslare Harbour to Waterford and Limerick train, hauled by a GM '141' Class Bo-Bo, pulls out of Campile in August 1976.

Right A hopeful backpacker studies the timetable at Rosslare Strand in August 2005. The time being 2pm, he has another 4hr 40min before the next train, the 17.30 from Waterford, followed hard on its heels by the only other train of the day, the 18.58 from Waterford (17.15 from Limerick Junction). The semaphore signals are still on duty.

Below A view from the evening Waterford to Rosslare boat train as it curves into Rosslare Strand station in August 1976.

Above The evening boat train, hauled by a GM Bo-Bo, approaches Rosslare Harbour in August 1976.

Right The metal destination boards on preserved CIE Park Royal 'laminate' Open 3rd No 1483 of 1955 were a feature of CIE main-line trains in the 1950s and '60s.

Below Passengers from the *Avalon*, just arrived from Fishguard, cross the track at Rosslare Harbour in August 1976.

Above An '001' Class Co-Co pulls out of Rosslare for Dublin in August 1988.

Below Seen from the ferry from Fishguard as it prepares to tie up at Rosslare Europort in July 2004, the two Craven carriages, Passenger Brake and GM Bo-Bo will form the 20.30 train to Waterford.

Above Beyond the Rosslare lifeboat, IR air-conditioned carriages are ready to form the 18.55 train to Dublin in July 2004.

Below Less than two weeks later DMUs took over the Dublin service, not to everyone's satisfaction for capacity was much reduced and at times there was considerable overcrowding. A four-car set is seen in July 2005, surrounded on three sides by water.

Above At Wexford South in August 1969 two elderly GSWR non-corridor carriages, with a four-wheel 'tin van' uncomfortably sandwiched between them, form the 11.30 service from Wexford North to Rosslare Harbour. The train is pausing for 1 minute before continuing its 9¾-mile journey, which, with further stops at Rosslare Strand and Kilrane, will take 43 minutes, 11 minutes of which will be taken up by the walking-pace negotiation of the three-quarters of a mile between the two Wexford stations. Wexford South closed in 1977.

Below The section of railway between Wexford North and Wexford South has always been a great source of interest to both enthusiasts and the general public – sometimes a source of annoyance to impatient members of the latter, running as it does along the water's edge and amongst the traffic. In this June 1958 picture the 11.30 Dublin to Rosslare train is in the charge of '101' Class 0-6-0 No 116. The four elderly carriages, including one Full Brake, are not likely to overtax the engine. *Brian Connell*

Above In 1969, 11 years after the previous picture, a diesel has charge of a vastly more modern rake of carriages tip-toeing along between a lightship and a row of cars, which includes the inevitable Beetle.

Below As can be seen in this August 2005 picture, the quay has been extended seawards so that the railway is now some distance from the water's edge.

Top and middle The distinctive signal box at the end of the footbridge at Arklow station, and up and down 29000 Class DMUs meeting, in August 2005.

Below A Dublin-Rosslare train, hauled by a General Motors 'B141' Class Co-Co, is deep in the woods of the Vale of Avoca between Arklow and Rathdrum in April 1985.

Above At Woodenbridge Junction on 28 June 1938 'D4' 4-4-0 No 335 is seen in the distance approaching with the 8.20am Rosslare Harbour to Dublin Harcourt Street train. *H. C. Casserley*

Below DMU No 29420, forming the 18.55 service from Rosslare Europort, nears the site of Woodenbridge station, now quite vanished, as it speeds by on its way to Dublin in August 2005.

Above Woodenbridge was the junction for the 16¾-mile-long branch to Shillelagh. Standing somewhat dwarfed by the not particularly long platform at Shillelagh on 28 June 1938 are two carriages and the locomotive of the 10.00am train to Woodenbridge. *H. C. Casserley*

Below This closer view of the complete train shows that it now consists of the two six-wheel carriages, three good wagons, and the locomotive, 'J15' No 174. *H. C. Casserley*

Above Although the last passenger train ran in 1944, goods ending a year later, much remained at Shillelagh in August 2005. This is the station house, now re-christened 'Camelot', which was just visible behind the station itself in the upper picture on the previous page.

Below The station building and the platform are also still clearly identifiable today. The goods shed, a little further on, is now in use as a GAA sports pavilion.

Above In this mid-1920s view Rathdrum station is dominated by the hotel, built by the D&SER, and a favourite with prosperous Dubliners who would come by train to take a break in the picturesque, wooded Vale of Avoca. *Lens of Sutton Collection*

Below Preserved former Dublin & South Eastern Railway 2-6-0 No 461 takes on water at the south end of Rathdrum station in August 1993. One of a pair of locomotives built by Beyer Peacock in 1922, No 461 was regularly employed for 40 years hauling the heaviest goods train between Rosslare, Wexford and Dublin, although it also put in appearances on passenger workings from time to time. Preserved as a non working exhibit in 1962, it lurked in various locations, mostly hidden away from public view, until being taken to the headquarters of the Railway Preservation Society of Ireland at Whitehead and returned to steam.

Below In August 1976 two of the original General Motors 950hp single-cab Bo-Bos of 1960 are about to depart with a Rosslare-Dublin train. By this date the station hotel had long been abandoned and stands gaunt and derelict. Tunnels mark the approach to Rathdrum from both north and south.

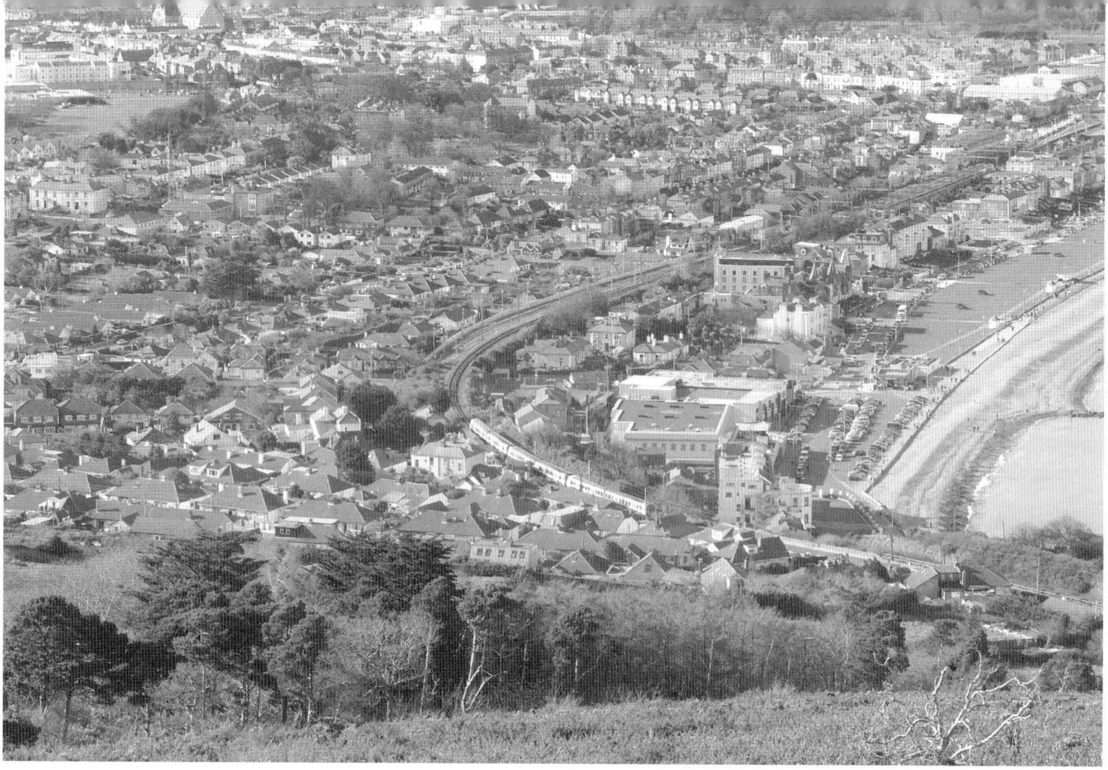

Above In this view from Bray Head looking north over the town on 27 March 2008, the station is in the top right on the picture; in the bottom right the six-car 14.48 service from Gorey to Dublin Connolly, formed of three 2700 units, is curving round the single-track section from the south on its approach to the station.

Below The south end of Bray station is seen on 17 August 1957 looking towards Bray Head on the horizon. On the left is 0-6-2T No 673, and on the right 0-6-0 No 89, behind which an 'A' Class diesel-electric in its original silver livery is shunting wagons while an AEC/Park Royal DMU is standing outside the shed, waiting to return to Dublin. No 673 is a rare beast in the sense that it is one of the few locomotives built by the GSR between 1925 and 1945; there were five of them, constructed at Inchicore in 1933 for Dublin suburban services. No 89 is a former GSWR Aspinall 4-4-0 of 1885/95. *C. H. A. Townley*

Above Dublin & South Eastern Railway 4-4-0 No 56 *Rathmines* waits at Bray on 21 July 1914 with the 3.00pm train from Harcourt Street. This locomotive was built by the Vulcan Foundry in 1895, reboilered in 1911, and withdrawn by the GSR in 1934. *LCGB, Ken Nunn Collection*

Below No 14, a D&SER 0-6-0 of 1905, stands on Bray shed on 25 May 1924. Despite being a humble goods engine, albeit one of a class that for nearly 30 years was the only Irish engine with a window cab, it was named *Limerick*, although one has to wonder why, seeing that this city was remote from D&SER territory. Built by the D&SER in its cramped Grand Canal Street Works, it lasted until 1955. *LCGB, Ken Nunn Collection*

Above left A view from Killiney station looking north in September 1967 as an 'A' Class approaches with a stopping train from Dublin to Bray.

Left A 'Sea Breeze' excursion composed of Railway Preservation Society of Ireland carriages hauled by former NCC 2-6-4T No 4 is at the summit of the climb from Killiney on 29 July 2007, passing some of the most desirable – and expensive – property in Europe.

Above In July 2006 a Dublin-bound DART, No 8639, built by Tokyu in Japan the previous year, on its way from Bray, climbs past Killiney along perhaps the most spectacular section of railway on the east coast.

Right Arrival at Glenageary, between Dalkey and Dun Laoghaire, on a summer evening in 2005.

Kingstown – such a name is loaded with connotations. Long known throughout Ireland as the stronghold of the West Britons, it is not surprising that the country's first railway ran the 6 miles from Dublin to here, where the steamer carrying the mail from London docked. Dun Laoghaire, to give the town its ancient and modern name, has always been a cosmopolitan sort of place, the first and last of Ireland for many passing through it. There is more than one view of it.

Plans were afoot from the earliest times, from the very dawn of the steam railway, for a line to Kingstown. Because the entry to Dublin Harbour could be extremely hazardous, there being only a narrow channel between sandbanks, a new, safer harbour was planned some 200 years ago further down the coast. The foundation stone was laid in 1817, and when King George IV visited Dunleary, as the original settlement was known, the name was changed to Kingstown. In February 1831, just two years after the first totally steam-worked public railway, the Liverpool & Manchester, had opened, a bill for the Dublin & Kingstown Railway was presented to the Westminster Parliament. Charles Vignoles was the engineer and William Dargan the contractor. Both were men of great distinction. The line was to be 5 miles 43 chains 4 yards long. Work began on 11 April 1833, and because for much of its length it was to run along the shores of Dublin Bay a great deal of work had to be done to ensure the trackbed was stable. This was achieved and on 31 July 1834 the line was declared complete and the directors travelled over it in a horse-drawn carriage, the first steam locomotives having not yet arrived. These were delivered early in the autumn, three from Sharp Brothers of Manchester and three from George Forrester of Liverpool. On 9 December 1834 regular traffic began, the first train departing from Westland Row at 9am, hauled by *Hibernia*, a Sharp 2-2-0. To quote the words of Kevin Murray, 'The opening was graced by no ceremony, as befitted a concern promoted, built and operated by businessmen.'

However, the line had not yet reached Kingstown Harbour, where the packets and mail boats from Holyhead now arrived, having deserted their previous port of Howth. This extension was completed and the first train, a non-stop one conveying the Lord Lieutenant, ran on 13 May 1837, 38 days before the accession of Queen Victoria, the journey from Westland Row taking a mere 13 minutes.

The Kingstown Railway was popular from the start. To quote Kevin Murray again:

'…the directors showed that they understood the value of service, by providing trains at regular intervals. They grasped the simple commercial policy – that regular, constant customers would be eminently the source of profit, when led out of the city to reside in a region of sea and country air, assuring the company of their daily business. As every vacant seat was a reproach to the management, a carriage filled with passengers at moderate rates was better … than a thinly occupied one at high fares.'

Large numbers of excursionists were conveyed on Sundays and before long trains were running every 15 minutes.

The next extension was 1¾ miles to Dalkey, where there were stone quarries, which were expected to provide lucrative business. This stretch was built as a revolutionary new form of transport, the atmospheric railway. A demonstration of this had been watched by the directors in London in 1840 and so impressed were they that they adopted it. Essentially what happened was that a cast-iron pipe was laid between the tracks, and an arm from a carriage connected to a piston inside the pipe, the arm passing along a slit in the top of the pipe, sealed fore and aft of the arm by a flexible flap; air was drawn out of the pipe and the vacuum created drew along the piston, and thus the arm and the carriage, and any others attached to it. Its application to the Kingstown to Dalkey railway was seen as a demonstration by its makers and promoters; much interest was created and many came to watch. Among them was I. K. Brunel, who adopted the system for the GWR in Devon. In theory it was utterly brilliant, involving little pollution – steam-powered pump houses were needed – it was remarkably quiet and trains could go as fast uphill as on the level.

But ultimately it failed. The Dalkey pump house burned more coal than if steam locomotives had been employed, the system broke down from time to time, which meant that, unlike on a conventional railway, everything ground to a halt, and it proved impossible to keep the pipe perfectly sealed, so there was a huge waste of power. Nevertheless it operated from August 1843 until April 1854. Subsequently much work had to be done to convert the line to steam operation and connect it at either end with the rest of the railway system, which was completed the following year. Very little evidence of its existence remains, perhaps the best known being Atmospheric Road, which runs alongside the cutting between Dalkey and Glenageary stations and which I walk past every time I make my way from my mother-in-law's house to Dalkey village. It is perhaps surprising that, with the 21st century's concern over pollution and global warming, serious attempts have not been made, using modern technology, to perfect what would seem to be a potentially wonderful mode of transport. The Dublin & Kingstown Railway and that from Kingstown to Dalkey had been built to a gauge of 4ft 8½in, which was standard in England, Wales and Scotland, but 5ft 3in had subsequently become the Irish standard, so in October 1855 the line between Westland Row and Dalkey adopted it.

The Great Western Railway now enters our story yet again. The company planned a new port in South Wales and a steamer service to what would become Rosslare, and a group of directors, including I. K. Brunel, came over in 1844 and suggested that the Dublin & Kingstown might like to establish a railway connection between Dublin and the proposed County Wexford port. Part of this cunning plan was to take some of the Anglo-Irish traffic away from the London & North Western Railway, as it would become through amalgamation in 1846. As it happened it would take some 60 years for the Fishguard-Rosslare route to come into existence. Nevertheless the GWR invested in a company called the Waterford, Wexford, Wicklow & Dublin Railway, which had Brunel as its engineer, and in August 1847 work began on building a railway from Dalkey to Bray. The Dublin & Kingstown Railway directors had previously agreed to lease their line to the WWW&DR, but had not yet officially handed it over.

As we have seen, progress was slow – Ireland was in the grip of the Great Famine – but trains began to run between Dublin and Bray in October 1855, and Rosslare was reached in 1882. Meanwhile the Dublin, Dundrum & Rathfarnham Railway proposed to build a rival, inland, route between Dublin and Bray, which would eventually became the Harcourt Street line. The Waterford, Wexford, Wicklow & Dublin, forced by financial stringency to restrain its ambitions, in 1851 renamed itself simply the Dublin & Wicklow. The DD&R, not exactly flush with funds, also changed its name, to the Dublin & Bray Railway, passed into the hands of the Dublin & Wicklow Railway, and opened between Harcourt Road, Dublin, and Shanganagh Junction, where it connected with the coast line, in July 1854. In 1859 it was extended the quarter-mile to Harcourt Street terminus.

A boat train stands in the bay platform at Dun Laoghaire on 27 April 1957. The locomotive is former GSWR Aspinall 'D14' Class 4-4-0 No 62 of 1885-95, and the first two carriages vastly more modern Bulleid-designed Open 2nds. *Hugh Davies*

Above A train of wooden-bodied carriages stands at the platform at Carlisle Pier, Dun Laoghaire, in about 1925. Alongside are two former LNWR mailboats, probably the *Hibernia* and *Cambria* (there was also the *Scotia*), built on the Clyde by Denny Brothers in 1920/1. *Author's collection*

Below At the same location in August 1969, the LMS-designed mail boat *Cambria*, ordered from Harland & Wolff in 1946 and successor to the LNWR vessel of the same name, is alongside the pier while 'C' Class No 211 is about to set off with the boat train for Dublin Pearse.

Above Successor of the LMS-designed *Cambria* was the *St Columba*, also seen docked in Dun Laoghaire in 1994. Built in 1977, she could carry 2,400 passengers and 334 cars. If you were very unlucky it was possible to stretch the normal 3½-hour voyage on the *St Columba* to 17 hours or even, if the Irish Sea had really got it in for you, an half hour short of a complete day, especially if you were silly enough to attempt the crossing in December. On the first occasion your author experienced a force 12 gale, on the night the Penlee lifeboat was lost with its entire crew, on the second the storm was most inconsiderably blowing straight up the Irish Sea, thus hitting the *St Columba* side on every time the captain attempted to dock at Holyhead. We saw an awful lot of Holyhead Bay that night and day! By the time this picture was taken *St Columba* had become *Stena Columba* and was shortly to be withdrawn.

Below The *Stena Adventurer*, the largest ferry ever to operate on the Irish Sea, passes Howth Head inward-bound from Holyhead in August 2006.

The final first-generation Dublin trams connected the city centre with Dun Laoghaire and Dalkey. After they finished on 9 July 1949 the Directors' tram was bought by a solicitor and placed in a rural oasis, shared with several pigs, in Barnhill Road, Glenageary, just up the hill from the Dalkey depot. Dating from 1901, it survived into the 1980s, absolutely complete if a little less than pristine until, even while negotiations were under way for its removal to the Howth Museum, vandals set it on fire. It is seen here shortly before that sad day. The remains were taken away but much restoration will be needed.

However, the preservationists, with very little official support but much encouraged by a few enthusiasts, of which perhaps the most notable is Michael Corcoran, have saved and restored several Dublin cars. This is No 224, a tram with a most interesting history. Originally T24, built in London in 1914 as a trailer car to operate for the LCC, it migrated across the Irish Sea, was found in a field in Abbeyleix and has been rebuilt as a Dublin open-top, open-front four-wheeler, a number of such cars having, indeed, been converted from trailers. It is seen here, posed in the city centre in 2004.

DUBLIN

Harcourt Street

Harcourt Street, designed by George Wilkinson, followed the pattern of all the Dublin termini by flattering to deceive, in that the approaching customer would have looked up and thought, 'Oh, by Jove, this is quite something – if it's this grand on the outside, what must it be like within?' only to discover that the answer was, 'Not much.' Jeanne Sheehy, writing in the Journal of the Irish Railway Record Society in 1975, describes its 'impressive Doric colonnade', and reminds us that the engineer, W. R. LeFanu, was a pupil of Sir John Macneill 'and brother of the novelist J Sheridan LeFanu', which is certainly a name to conjure with, although possibly not as familiar to 21st-century readers as, say, Roddy Doyle or Maeve Binchy. Miss Sheehy also alludes to the 'bold curve of the shed', which is somewhat puzzling as, although I never travelled from the station, none of the pictures I have ever seen of its single-platform interior feature much in the way of curves, bold or otherwise; perhaps she was referring to the end wall. To quote Brian Mac Aongusa in his *Harcourt Street Line* (Currach Press, 2003), 'Dubliners referred to it as an egg – "a lovely shell on the outside with just a yolk (yoke) inside."'

Much has been written on the Harcourt Street line, particularly of late with LUAS taking over much of its trackbed, and today it seems extraordinary that a railway serving the Dublin suburbs, the fastest train connecting Bray with the city in just 23 minutes, could ever have been considered redundant. Yet such it was, and the last train departed from Harcourt Street station at 2.40pm on 1 January 1959.

No 436, a former D&SER 'F1' Class 2-4-2T of 1901-9, pulls out of Harcourt Street on 16 May 1950 with the 3.20pm to Greystones. The line of veteran six-wheelers sunning themselves in the sidings may have had something to do with patrons deserting the railway for the new Leyland Titan double-deck buses. *H. C. Casserley*

Harcourt Street was at one time the terminus of boat trains from Kingstown, although once the Loop Line was opened it was more convenient to take them to Westland Row where connections could be made with the rest of the rail network. On 24 May 1924 D&SER 4-4-0 No 55 *Rathdown* stands outside Harcourt Street. *LCGB, Ken Nunn Collection*

The 2pm to Bray, in the charge of 'J19' No 603, a former MGWR 0-6-0 of 1885-9, is about to depart from Harcourt Street on 25 April 1955. *H. C. Casserley*

Traffic on the Harcourt Street line gradually declined until it was closed at the beginning of 1959, but as the area it had served began to become built up, it was not long before the folly of this came to be generally recognised. However, it was more than four decades before restoration came in the shape of Dublin's LUAS tram system, which opened on 20 June 2004, using some 70 per cent of the old Harcourt Street trackbed. A city-bound tram is seen at Dundrum, the only original station still surviving in the summer of 2005, although not used by LUAS passengers.

Terenure

The Dublin & Blessington Tramway ran from Terenure, in the suburbs of south-west Dublin, to Blessington, 15 miles distant at the foot of the Dublin mountains; at Terenure connection was made with the Dublin tram system. It opened in 1888, and an extension to Poulaphouca was opened in 1890, and closed in 1928. The main line closed in 1932.

Above A petrol-engined railbus, tram No 5 (which would be hauled by a curious double-cab 2-4-2T steam engine), two cyclists, two other bystanders and several wagons are seen at Terenure on 17 September 1929. *H. C. Casserley*

Below left Buses replaced the Dublin & Blessington trams on the first day of 1933. A Dublin Bus Bombardier double-decker heads through the Co Dublin countryside towards Blessington in December 1991.

Below Today Dublin Bus route 15B connects Terenure with the city centre. Alexander-bodied Volvo AX473 double-deckers, two of which are seen in the city on 27 July 2006, operate the route.

Westland Row/Pearse and the Loop Line

If Harcourt Street did not take their fancy, travellers from the south had the alternative of arriving at Westland Row. Rather nearer the city centre, from 1891 it offered the additional advantage of taking passengers deeper into the heart of Dublin by way of Tara Street station on the Quays, across the River Liffey, past the back door of the Customs House, and on to Amiens Street, to a separate station alongside the GNR's terminus. This was the property of the City of Dublin Junction Railway, popularly known as the Loop Line. A mere mile in length, it is impossible to underestimate its value, providing a link with every railway serving the capital, and today the vital heart of the ever-increasing suburban network, without which Dublin would, at times, probably grind to a halt. The business section of Westland Row, like Amiens Street and Harcourt Street, was upstairs. Unlike the others, the two through platforms and the three bays are protected from the weather not by pitched roofs but a much loftier arched one. Another entrance, reached by a sloping drive for horse carriage access, faced in the direction of the Liffey on the down side, but today everyone uses the Westland Row entrance and gains the platforms by escalators. Westland Road station was renamed Pearse in 1966.

Tara Street has no pretensions to architectural merit, consisting merely of two rather narrow platforms, reached, like Pearse, by escalators, but it does tremendous business, being in the heart of the city, and is the busiest station in Ireland.

As part of a recreation of Ireland's first public railway service in Dalkey Museum, *Hibernia* pulls the 9am train to Kingstown out of Westland Row on Wednesday 17 December 1834.

One of the original DARTs arrives at Pearse station, as Westland Row became in 1966, on its way to Dun Laoghaire and Bray in July 2006.

Above D&SER 2-4-2T No 433, an 1898 rebuild of one of the company's standard 2-4-0Ts, stands outside Grand Canal Street depot in about 1950. *Author's collection*

Below Today Grand Canal Dock station stands on the site, serving the ever-increasing number of high-rise offices and desirable residences in an area of Dublin that not so long ago was much less desirable. A DMU is standing in the station, and underneath is the arch that spans the Grand Canal itself, with a glimpse of old Dublin beyond and the Dublin Mountains in the distance.

IRELAND'S RAILWAY HERITAGE: LEINSTER

By the late 1960s CIE's carriage fleet had been very much modernised and nearly all the old wooden-bodied vehicles from pre-Great Southern days had gone. However, until 1972 a fleet of some 50 former GSWR and very early GSR carriages was retained as secondary stock, re-numbered in the 4xxx series. One rake, which became quite celebrated, appeared for several summers on Dublin suburban services. Most of its carriages were non-corridor vehicles, and it is seen here crossing the Liffey and entering Tara Street station on its way to Bray in the summer of 1969.

CIE's AEC/Park Royal diesel railcars were bought with the intention of using them on long-distance workings, and this they did throughout the 1950s and on some routes into the 1960s. Some went straight into suburban work around Dublin and eventually, as more and more diesel-electric locomotives entered service and steam disappeared, so the rest followed suit. In this picture, taken from the roof of Liberty Hall in 1967, a seven-coach railcar set, still on long-distance duties, is on the Loop Line just a couple of minutes from the end of its journey from Sligo to Pearse station.

• 104 •

Amiens Street/Connolly and North Wall

Amiens Street, renamed Connolly in 1966, a few hundred yards from Westland Row across the Liffey, is, as we have noted, two stations in one, an extensive, complex establishment, parts of which, like practically every piece of GNR architecture, inherited or built, have real merit. The Italianate tower facing Talbot Street is a notable landmark, even if it is somewhat overshadowed by the extensive office buildings that have shot up and continue to appear, almost overnight it seems, in the modern, thrusting, dynamic Dublin! Amiens Street had the great advantage over the city's other principal terminus, the Great Southern & Western's Kingsbridge, of being much nearer the city centre. It is only in recent times that the latter has catered for commuter traffic, while it has always been a feature at Amiens Street.

Amiens Street station was the work of William Deane Butler, and was completed for the Dublin & Drogheda Railway in 1846, so it actually pre-dates the GNR by 30 years. The platforms are a considerable height above the street and were reached by a flight of 22 steps, presenting, in the words of E. M. Patterson, ' a formidable barrier to luggage porters on their way to the platform'. Eventually the GNR built a sloping roadway up to the concourse, which made life a lot easier for everyone. Some 120 years later this was removed, involving much excavation, so that the LUAS trams could terminate immediately below Connolly station, two flights of escalators and a lift carrying passengers – where have all the porters gone? – smoothly hither and thither. Sheriff Street passes beneath the station and the four platforms are supported by 22 cast iron columns, supplied by Coalbrookdale in 1844. The Coalbrookdale works, based in the Severn Valley in Shropshire where the Industrial Revolution began, must surely be the oldest working ones in the world, for they have been in production for more than 200 years. Across Sheriff Street – where a wooden sign pointing to the GNR goods yard lasted well into the 1990s – the Dublin & Drogheda Railway built its equally impressive, equally Italianate head offices of Wicklow granite, which are used today by Iarnrod Eireann.

Behind them the Loop Line curves into its station, opened in 1891 by the City of Dublin Junction Railway. This has three through platforms and was operated as a completely separate establishment, reached by an entrance in Amiens Street and a long slope and steps. There was a wooden footbridge at the far end of the station, which connected the two establishments. I was never quite sure in its later years, when the two stations were connected in other ways and were treated as one, whether it was intended to be used by the public, but although hardly a thing of beauty it was a splendid vantage point to watch the trains coming and going and no-one ever shooed me off it. Eventually it was closed and removed.

Immediately beyond the end of the GNR platforms is an engine shed, rather like the English GNR set-up at King's Cross. However, the Irish GNR one survives to this day, is home to diesel locomotives and also sometimes to one of the Railway Preservation Society of Ireland's steam locomotives, which call in and on occasions take up temporary residence there. I can't think offhand of anywhere else in Ireland or the UK where the once common sight of locomotives entering or leaving their depot can be seen from the platform ends of a main-line station.

The GNR trains head north over the Royal Canal, and the former MGWR line to the North Wall goods depot and the docks, and now to the new Docklands passeger station. There is a wonderfully complex series of lines and junctions hereabouts. There are connections between the former GNR tracks and the Loop Line ones immediately beyond Connolly station. Two lines curve away sharply and steeply from the Loop Line tracks down to Newcomen Junction where they join the former MGWR tracks in the direction of Glasnevin Junction and all points west. A little further on a second pair of double tracks, built by the CDJR in 1906, curve away almost as sharply, and join the former GSWR line from North Wall at North Strand Junction. These also head for Glasnevin Junction. Returning to the former GNR lines, the next junction is at East Wall, where yet another line from North Wall comes in. Immediately afterwards the River Tolka passes beneath on its way into Dublin Bay, then on the left is Fairview Depot, originally erected by the GNR for its railcars and much enlarged and modernised over the years to accommodate the ever-expanding DART fleet of EMUs. Once Dublin Bay came right up to the trackside, but the land has been reclaimed and on part of it the new station of Clontarf Road, dating from 2000, has been built. There was an earlier station, a wooden halt, in the vicinity, which closed in 1956 and could hardly be compared with the state-of-the-art modern station with its lifts and extensive car park.

North Wall has always been much the busiest goods depot in Ireland, although today that is not saying much. The complex of lines and depots was owned chiefly by the GSWR – although the MGWR, the GNR and even the LNWR staked their claims – and there was a time when passenger trains served it. These finished originally in the early 1920s but returned in 2007 with a new terminus at Spencer Dock, on the site of the former MGWR depot, to serve commuter traffic from the Maynooth line. Passenger carriages have always been in evidence at North Wall, either dumped in sidings after withdrawal, converted after their passenger-carrying days to serve in departmental use, new vehicles being unloaded from ships, and, recently, DART vehicles awaiting loading aboard a vessel for overhaul and upgrading. As I write there are still a good many lines and sidings at North Wall, and a fair collection of freight wagons, much of it out of use, but most of this is likely to disappear unless something remarkable happens and the Government and the Board of Iarnrod Eireann take fright at being labelled the only developed country in the European Union where freight traffic is declining as rapidly as it is increasing everywhere else. An interesting re-use of the Point, a former GSWR granite-built goods depot, is as a venue for pop concerts and theatrical performances.

The impressive buildings of the GNR's Amiens Street terminus, Connolly since 1966, in the summer of 2006. Beyond is the not dissimilar Italianate Dublin & South Eastern Railway station tower.

Right Amiens Street station in June 1961, with two far from run-of-the-mill modes of road transport. *John Parker*

Right No 4, a Dublin, Wicklow & Wexford 2-2-2WT of 1879, is seen at Amiens Street on 2 September 1901. Built by the company at Grand Canal Street, it was withdrawn in 1908. *LCGB, Ken Nunn Collection*

Below Almost brand-new No 172, a GNR Clifford-designed 'S' Class 4-4-0, pulls out of Amiens Street with the 9am express to Belfast on 22 July 1914. *LCGB, Ken Nunn Collection*

Above The final design of 4-4-0, anywhere in the world, was the 'VS' Class, a most handsome variation of the pre-war Compound 4-4-0s. Designed by McIntosh and built for the GNR in Manchester by Beyer Peacock in 1948, No 208 *Lagan* is seen outside Amiens Street shed in June 1961. Behind is No 48, an 'SG3' 0-6-0 of 1920/1. *John Parker*

Below 'Q' Class 4-4-0 No 132 of 1899-1904, a Great Northern engine in CIE ownership, stands beside the distinctive signal box on the Great Southern side of Amiens Street station on 3 June 1961 with an IRRS special for Navan and Kingscourt. *David Lawrence*

UTA 2-6-4T No 56 has arrived at Connolly on 4 May 1968 with an RPSI special from Belfast. For a short while at the end of the steam era one of these highly successful express tank engines was attached to a tender and employed on through Belfast-Dublin trains, but the experiment was not pursued. *David Lawrence*

'071' Class Co-Co No 082 was given a splendid new livery, primarily of silver and black, after overhaul at Inchicore in the spring of 2007, and named *The Institution of Engineers of Ireland*. It is seen here about to depart from Connolly with the 17.05 service to Sligo on 3 August 2007, its carriages consisting of about-to-be-withdrawn BREL modified Mark 2s of 1972.

22000 Class Korean-built Rotem long-distance railcars were put on to the Dublin-Sligo route at the beginning of 2008. A vastly improved service every 2 hours saw a substantial rise in patronage and a very high passenger approval response. The six-car 19.05 to Sligo is seen here on the right, with the 19.00 'Enterprise' service to Belfast in its new livery on the left, at Connolly on 27 March 2008.

A brave and innovative attempt to provide Dublin with an electric suburban train service without the need either for overhead wires or a third rail was the Drumm battery system, the brainchild of a Dublin University professor, Dr Drumm. In all, four battery-powered units were built between 1932 and 1939, and each unit could cover 80 miles between re-charging. They continued to work until 1949-50. This is unit B, composed of two handsome-looking vehicles, built at Inchicore and seen at Amiens Street. Note the destination boards beneath the cab windows and the battery boxes attached to the underframes, extending from bogie to bogie. The unit is coupled to a non-corridor carriage painted, like unit B, in the attractive dark brown and cream livery used for a time by the GSR on its more favoured bogie carriages. *Lens of Sutton Collection*

Railcar G was one of the somewhat unusual but nevertheless successful three-car railcars of the GNR that had a central power bogie, driven by a Gardner 102hp diesel engine. The two lightweight coaches flanking it seated between them some 150 passengers. The 19-year-old unit is arriving at Amiens Street from Howth on 1 August 1957. *Norman Simmons*

No 29120 brings up the rear of one of the Spanish-built four-car DMUs, introduced by IR in 2001, heading out of Connolly for Dundalk in December 2004.

DUBLIN

Right A LUAS tram has just left Connolly on its way to Tallaght and is about to pass under an IR DMU that has also just left Connolly on its way to Tara Street and Pearse in August 2005. With the opening of Dublin's new tram network, Connolly and Heuston stations are directly connected by the Red Line, which begins at Connolly, passes the Central Bus Station, Busaurus, then curves around the back of the Customs House, as in this picture. It then heads along Abbey Street, over O'Connell Street and runs parallel with the Quays until crossing the Liffey by Heuston Bridge to Heuston station, then up beside the Guinness Brewery and on through the suburbs to Tallaght.

Right Three of the French-built Citaris LUAS trams are seen in Abbey Street in July 2006. The LUAS network is built to the standard European gauge of 4ft 8½in, as is the planned Metro.

Below B101, one of the CIE diesel-electric locomotives built by BRCW in 1955-57 and fitted with Sulzer 960hp engines delivered several years earlier and intended for six twin-engined locomotives, heads through Glasnevin Junction on 25 April 1973 with a freight train from North Wall.

Above No 264, a big former GSWR 'J4' 0-6-0 of 1913/4, shunts cattle wagons at North Wall in about 1960. The cattle trade provided Irish railways with much business in those days, many of the animals being shipped from North Wall and elsewhere to the UK. *Hugh Davies*

Below This is the former GSWR yard at North Wall in 1978, with an '001' Class Co-Co and an 'E' Class shunter. Beyond the cranes and masts are the twin chimneys of the Pigeon House power station, situated on the south bank of the Liffey.

On a very wet August afternoon in 2004, CAF carriages are being unloaded at North Wall from the *Flintersprint*, which has brought them from Spain. GM Bo-Bo No 147 waits to haul them up to Inchicore.

Two views of the new Docklands station, shortly after being opened on 12 March 2007 by the Taoiseach, Bertie Ahern. Built on the site of the former Midland goods depot, the project cost 20 million euros, was opened three months ahead of schedule and was under budget. Serving the new business district based along the north bank of the Liffey, it will enable 2,500 more commuters to arrive in the heart of the city each day. It is served by 15 trains each way, which make the 20-minute journey to Clonsilla, out in the western suburbs on the Midland line, in addition to the already established service to Connolly station. The train is a brand-new Japanese-built Rotem railcar.
Michael Walsh

Broadstone

Broadstone, the MGWR's terminus, is as impressive a piece of railway architecture as you will find anywhere, although I ought to add a rider to the effect that it hasn't actually seen sight or sound of a train since 18 January 1937. On that date the last of its services, which had always been few and far between, were transferred to Amiens Street and Westland Row. John Skipton Mulvany was the MGWR's architect; he was paid £250 per annum in the 1840s, and Broadstone, his masterpiece, was completed in 1850. A guide to the railway described it thus: 'a chaste and truly noble erection in granite, combining in its details the peculiarities of the Egyptian and Grecian styles of architecture'. Another guide tells us that George Willoughby Hemans, engineer to the company, 'seems to have been involved in the design of the shed', and goes on to say as an aside that he was the 'son of Felicia Hemans, the Victorian poetess of note'.

The original two platforms proved more than adequate throughout the station's existence as a train terminus. In 1861 an immensely long and highly impressive colonnade was added on the arrival side sufficient to accommodate practically all the horse cabs in the city. Back in the 1960s I came across the preserved original Dublin Leyland Titan double-decker, R1, gathering dust there, quite dwarfed by its surroundings.

The station was built beside the Royal Canal, which, like the Grand Canal, linked Dublin with the River Shannon and thus the west coast. The Royal Canal had been completed in 1814, but the Grand had got there first, so the Royal never made a profit. It suited the MGWR to buy the Royal Canal, for £298,059, and for 34 miles build its line to the west alongside it. One of my favourite walks when my parents-in-law lived in Glasnevin was to walk up to the Brian Boru public house and follow the towpath along the canal, past a number of derelict, sunken barges and the North City Mills (which in the late 1960s was still served by a long siding off the MGWR Liffey branch), past a picturesque, single-storey lock-keeper's cottage, which looked as if it had strayed from a Paul Henry painting of Connemara, to Liffey Junction. Here the railway crossed to the other bank of the canal and met the line coming up the hill from Broadstone. This was still used then, bringing oil tankers for the provincial buses and coaches that had taken over Broadstone in the 1930s. The engine shed and the wagon repair shop had lasted until 1961. A signal box, into which I was on occasions invited, controlled the junction and the sidings, which were inhabited by time-expired goods wagons, and the occasional carriage, waiting to make their last journey to the breakers' yard at Mullingar. The platforms at Liffey Junction – and indeed the station nameboards proclaiming its title in both English and Irish – were still in place, although no ordinary passenger had alighted there since the closure of Broadstone; it had only ever been an exchange point. Now it is all gone, except for the canal and the main line.

Above right Connaught, a Midland Great Western 2-4-0, one of Martin Atock's standard express engines built from 1893, is seen at Broadstone when new. Atock fitted his engines with a highly distinctive 'fly-away' cab. Much rebuilt over the years, this class became the last active 2-4-0s either in Ireland or the UK, some surviving into the 1960s. MGWR locomotives tended to be very long-lived; of the 139 taken over by the GSR in 1925, 109 were still running at the creation of CIE 20 years later. *Author's collection*

Right Broadstone station closed on 18 January 1937. It survived as a locomotive depot into the 1960s, but eventually the entire establishment became the headquarters of the provincial bus fleet. A Bus Eireann coach, sporting the handsome Irish wolfhound logo, stands in the yard.

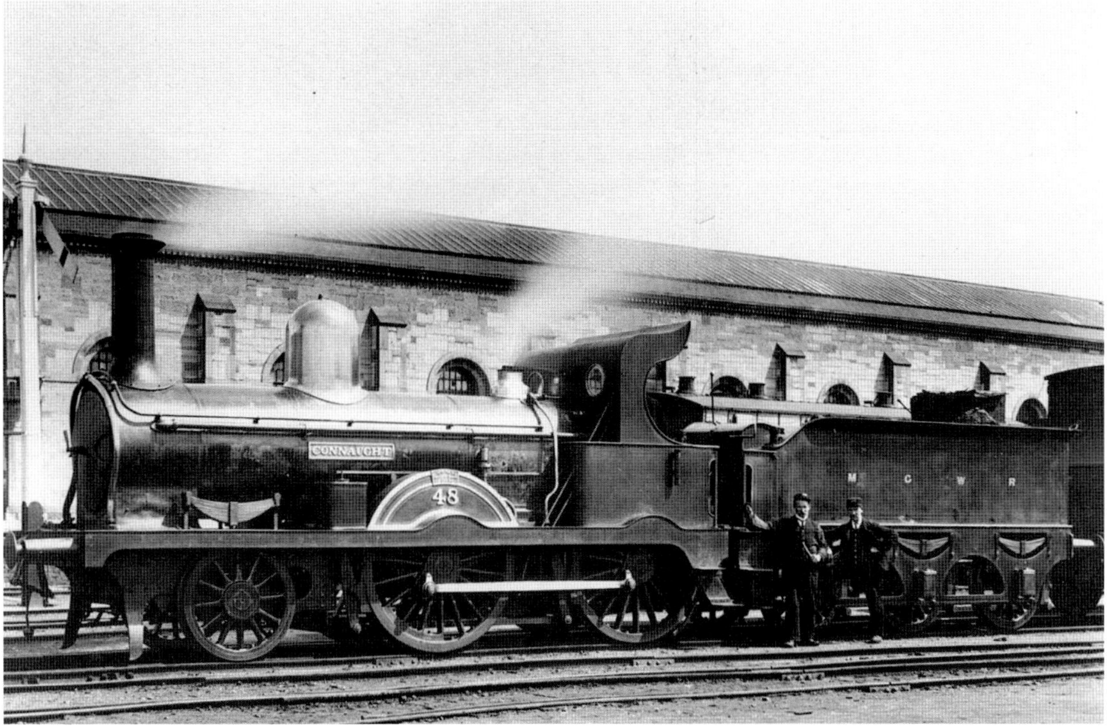
CONNAUGHT
48
M G W R

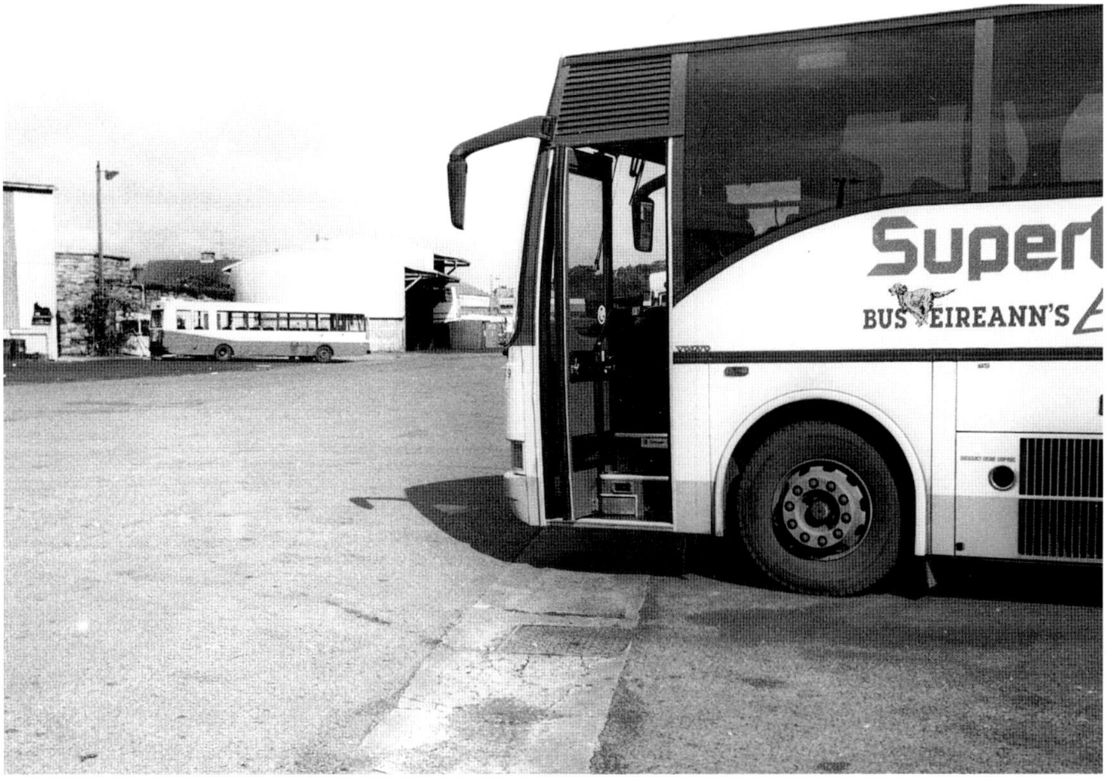
Super
BUS EIREANN'S

Ireland's Railway Heritage: Leinster

Above The MGWR bought the Royal Canal and for much of its distance its line to the west runs alongside it.

Liffey Junction was where the line from Broadstone met that from Islandbridge Junction to Amiens Street, along which trains were diverted when The Broadstone (the prefix was commonly applied) closed. This is a view taken in 1982 from the railway bridge spanning the canal, with semaphore signals prominent. Liffey Junction station was at this date still more or less intact. Much of the Midland's business was with cattle, and as late as the 1960s the author's wife can remember as a child on car outings to the Phoenix Park frequently being held up by herds of cows that had been unloaded at Liffey Junction and were being walked to the city's cattle market.

Left A single track ran down from Liffey Junction to Broadstone, and it lasted for many years after the last train had run. There is a possibility that it was used for a while to bring in oil for the buses, but there is some doubt about this. This picture dates from 1972.

Below Today wildlife, supermarket shopping trolleys and suchlike exotica have the trackbed to themselves, although the LUAS trams may one day bring back rail travel. For Midland-line trains the new Docklands station relieves some of the pressure on Connolly. Here a train from Clonsilla passes under another DMU on the approach to Connolly as it enters Docklands in August 2007.

Kingsbridge/Heuston

Kingsbridge was for much of its career not a lot busier than Broadstone. Neither had any commuter traffic and both were rather far from the city centre, the business sector had moved down the Quays towards O'Connell Street (Sackville Street as it was until 1924), while administrative, entertainment and visitor Dublin were all some distance away. Trains leaving Kingsbridge met the GSWR North Wall branch just beyond the station, which emerged from the Phoenix Park Tunnel and crossed the Liffey at Islandbridge Junction, then made the steep 1 in 117/84 climb past Inchicore Works, thus gaining open country but still climbing for 4½ miles to Clondalkin.

The transformation that has overtaken Heuston, as Kingsbridge became in 1966, at the end of the 20th and into the 21st centuries is remarkable. The two platforms, three if one counts the bay, have become eight, plus another, a through one, on the North Wall branch close to Islandbridge Junction, the freight yards have vanished, and there are now two concourses, one serving the new platforms 5-8, while the original one has been enlarged, lightened, had various facilities added and improved out of all recognition. And once again you can board a tram outside and be whisked, smoothly and in comfort, into the heart of the city.

The Loop Line connecting Connolly, Pearse and North Wall with Heuston, Islandbridge and Inchicore probably sees a greater variety of trains than any other part of the Irish railway system, and the metal footbridge spanning it between Drumcondra and Glasnevin has always provided a grandstand for trainspotters of all ages. This picture was taken in 1977.

The 08.30 Connolly to Sligo train passes under the footbridge in August 2004, a new one that replaced that in the previous picture in the late 1990s.

Former GSWR 'J4' No 258 stands at Islandbridge Junction on 27 April 1957, with the Liffey bridge and Phoenix Park Tunnel in the background. The three goods brake-vans in the foreground consist of a GNR vehicle just elbowing its way into the picture, a former GSWR wooden-bodied one, and the GSR metal-bodied version of the GSWR design. *Norman Simmons*

No A60R, a re-engined Metro-Vick Co-Co, emerges from the Phoenix Park Tunnel and crosses the River Liffey on the approach to Islandbridge Junction with a passenger train from Connolly in August 1972.

Two General Motors '141' Class Bo-Bos wait for the road to Inchicore at Islandbridge Junction in August 2003. At the time a vast updating and extension of Heuston station was in progress; the goods yard was disappearing, a new platform had been built beside where the two locomotives are standing, and the station was being completely remodelled.

• DUBLIN •

Above This is Kingsbridge station in about 1920. A train of GSWR carriages, most of them six-wheelers although there are also some bogie carriages, occupies the central tracks; these remained in use as carriage sidings until the 1970s, with only two main platforms, plus a shorter bay, available for arrivals and departures. *Author's collection*

Below At the same location, Heuston station, on 2 March 2008, General Motors 201 Class 3,200hp Co-C No 225 *River Deel/Abhainn Na Daoile*, stands ready t depart for the west.

Left Photographed at Heuston in August 2006 is the streamlined driving cab of CAF Spanish-built Driving Brake Generator Van No 4003, delivered in 2004 and designed, although not yet permitted, for a maximum speed of 125mph. Beyond is Brake Generator Van No 7606, one of the BREL Mark 3 vehicles of 1986.

Left No 234 *River Aherlow/ Abhainn Na Heathaplai* heads out of Heuston with the 19.00 service to Cork on 1 August 2007, passing No 213 *River Moy/Abhainn Na Muaidhe*.

Below left The interior of a Standard Class CAF carriage.

Below The modern refreshment area inside the much improved, enlarged and lightened concourse of Heuston, photographed in August 2005.

Above One of the large 'D2' 4-4-0s, built by Coey in 1904-6 for the GSWR, shunts the empty stock of a Cork express on 27 April 1957 – not the ideal locomotive, with its 6ft 7in driving wheels, for such a duty. The first vehicle is one of the almost new aluminium-liveried 'tin' four-wheel heating vans, and most of the carriages are modern vehicles dating from the 1950s, but the third vehicle is a 1915 vintage dining-car, built at Inchicore, one of a pair that had a very long career, lasting on front-line duties into the 1970s. The heating vans were given this extraordinarily impractical livery so that they would match the similarly adorned 'A' Class locomotives, one of which can be seen in the distance alongside the end of the train that it is probably going to take out later. *Brian Connell*

Below BRCW Sulzer-engined No B105 of 1956 and shunter No E414 of 1958 are at work in the freight yard at Heuston in August 1971. No B105 ceased work in November 1977 and was broken up at North Wall ten years later. No E414 stopped work a few months before B105 and was broken up at Inchicore in 1984.

Guinness operated an extensive system of narrow and standard gauge railways within its brewery and along the street to Kingsbridge station. In about 1960, while a horse and cart passes on its way towards the Quays, a diesel locomotive heads towards the Kingsbridge goods yard with a train of covered wagons, the first belonging to the GNR. *Hugh Davies*

Above A diesel-hauled train emerges from the Guinness works and prepares to negotiate its way between Ford (left) and Vauxhall saloons on 5 April 1963. *Hugh Davies*

Below A number of Guinness locomotives have been preserved. This is a narrow gauge one, at Amberley Working Museum in Sussex, in September 2006.

Inchicore Works

Located beside the Great Southern & Western main line west of Kingsbridge, this was successively the works of the GSWR, the Great Southern, CIE and Iarnrod Eireann.

Above In this 27 April 1957 view, with Inchicore Works just visible on the right, No 261, a commendably clean Coey 'J4' 0-6-0 of 1901/4, shunts the MGWR state saloon of 1903, complete with six-wheel bogies, and two brand-new aluminium brake-vans. No expense had been spared in the construction of the saloon, with its interior panelled by Millar & Beatty of Dublin, a dining saloon, galley and observation section. Sadly it was broken up in the 1960s.
Brian Connell

Below Undoubtedly the most famous Irish saloon of all time is No 351. Built by the GSWR at Inchicore in 1902, it originally had a clerestory roof, being rebuilt with an elliptical one in the 1920s. It remained in use for notable visitors, Taoiseachs and Presidents – I once saw President De Valera alight from it at Heuston in 1969 – until it was replaced by a modern air-conditioned vehicle and was set aside. It very nearly suffered the same fate as the MGWR carriage, but a concerted effort to rescue it began in the 1990s, one of the leading lights being Charles Meredith. Skilled craftsmen willingly lent their time and skills, grants were received, and eventually the President, Mary McAleese, presided over the ceremony at the culmination of its restoration. It is seen here, beautifully attired in GSR livery, at Inchicore on 21 December 2004.

Above A lengthy Cork express, consisting of mostly arc-roofed bogie carriages, but with at least one six-wheeler, climbs away past Inchicore Works in the charge of No 326, a '321' Class 4-4-0 of 1905, on 21 July 1914. *LCGB, Ken Nunn Collection*

Below Canadian-built '201' Class 3,200hp Co-Co No 212 *Abhainn Na Slanne/River Slaney* stands outside Inchicore, with the familiar backdrop of whitewashed terraced houses, in December 2004.

Above Among the locomotives in this picture of Inchicore running shed in about 1955 are several of the inevitable '101' 0-6-0s, including No 256, and, in the line on the left, a '400' Class 4-6-0. *Brian Connell*

Left '101' Class No 188 was photographed at Inchicore on 2 August 1901. It has the double smokebox doors that a few of the class retained throughout their careers, one or two into the 1960s. *LCGB, Ken Nunn Collection*

Left No 170 was another of this most famous of Irish steam locomotive classes, and is receiving attention at Inchicore on the same day. *LCGB, Ken Nunn Collection*

The GNR, strapped for money as it was after the initial immediate post-war investment in 15 steam locomotives, took the plunge and bought an 800hp diesel-hydraulic from MAK, Germany, in 1954. It was the company's only modern diesel locomotive. Passing to CIE in 1958, which renumbered it K801, it is seen at Inchicore in 1969. Withdrawn in 1976, it had a brief but presumably very satisfying second career powering a car-crushing plant at Galway Metals. However, the power unit ceased the following year. The remains of No K801 eventually succumbed in 1999.

The pioneer Sulzer-powered CIE diesel-electric locomotive No 1100, built at Inchicore in 1951, is at the head of down freight on 27 April 1957. *Norman Simmons*

One of the finest exhibits in Cultra, itself one of the finest of all transport museums, is this model of Inchicore depot. Depicted alongside the shed are two express passenger 4-6-0s, No 409, one of the originally unsuccessful Watson engines of 1921-2, later much rebuilt and used on Dublin-Cork expresses until replaced in the 1950s by diesels, and No 800 *Maeve* of 1939, Ireland's most famous, most powerful and fastest steam locomotive, now preserved at Cultra.

Index of photographic locations

Abbeyleix 66
Adamstown 54
Ardee 27
Arklow 85
Athboy 35
Athlone 46-47
Athy 61

Bagenalstown 64
Balbriggan 37
Ballybrophy 69-70
Beauparc 31
Birr 70
Bray 90-91
Brosna Halt 70

Campile 79
Carbury 44
Carlingford 25
Carlow 62-63
Cherryville Junction 59-60
Clara 49-50
Clonsilla 36

Deerpark Siding 66
Drogheda 29-31; Boyne Viaduct 28
Dromin Junction 27
Dublin & Blessington Tramway 101
Dublin, Amiens Street/Connolly 106-111
  Broadstone 115
  Docklands 113, 116
  Grand Canal Street 113
  Harcourt Street 99-100
  Islandbridge Junction 117-118
  Kingsbridge/Heuston 119-123
  North Wall 112-113
  Tara Street 104
  Terenure 101
  Westland Row/Pearse 102
Dun Laoghaire 95-97
Dunboyne 36
Dundalk 4, 14-19, 21-23; north of, near border 11-12

Edenderry 44

Glasnevin Junction 111
Glenageary 93
Goresbridge 74
Greenore 23-24
Guinness railway 122-123

Horseleap 48
Howth 40; Hill of Howth tramway 41
Howth Junction 39

Inchicore 124-127

Kells 32
Kilkenny 65
Killiney 92-93
Kilmainham Wood 34
Kilmessan Junction 35
Kingscourt 34
Kingstown *see* Dun Laoghaire

Liffey Junction, Dublin 116

Macmine Junction 76

Malahide 37-38
Mountmellick 68
Muine Bheag *see* Bagenalstown
Mullingar 45

Naas 57
Navan 32
New Ross 73-74
Newry 20, 25
Nobber 34

Oldcastle 33

Palace East 75-76
Portarlington 67-68

Raheny 42
Rathdrum 89
Rosslare Strand 79; Harbour 80-82

Sallins 54-57
Shillelagh 87-88
Streamstown 48
Sutton 68

Tullow 58

Waterford 72, 78
Wellington Bridge 78
Wexford 83-84
Wilkenstown 33
Wolfhill branch 62
Woodenbridge Junction 86